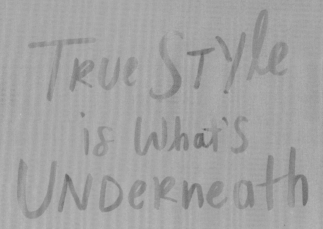

True STYLe
is What's
UNDeRneath

-:::::::::::-

THE SELF-Acceptance
REVOLUTION

Style That's Beneath

A StyleLikeU Manifesto
By Elisa Goodkind
and Lily Mandelbaum

THE SELF-Acceptance REVOLUTION

UNIVERSE

Contents

2.

Dress To
Express Your
Inner Spirit

54

3.

Consume
Consciously

90

6.

Embrace
your UNIQUE
Identity

196

7.

Create Your
own Definition
of Beauty

234

FOR NEARLY A DECADE, it has been our
Calling to UNCOVER what's underneath
authentic
style.

helping to build a world where
getting dressed each morning
is an act of self-love.

Elisa & Lily

STYLELIKEU FOUNDERS
NEW YORK

✦

Lily

Growing up, I struggled endlessly with my body image. In an oversaturated media culture dominated by women who looked nothing like me, I was consumed with trying to change myself physically in order to be and look like someone else. All the while, I was getting further out of touch with who I was.

Elisa

At the same time, I was working as a fashion stylist and, after twenty years in the business, I felt totally stuck. The industry, which had once left room for artistry and rebellion, had become about selling status, conformity and increasingly formulaic ideals of beauty. This oppressive culture was not only squashing my ability to express myself but it eventually hit me that it was also robbing my daughter of a healthy self-esteem.

Instead of accepting this status quo, we chose to create an alternative. That alternative was StyleLikeU.

They reminded us that being 'stylish' is not synonymous with being young, rich, thin, trendy or famous, that it is not necessarily about having a designer label or an 'it' bag. They taught us that true style is a reflection of the nonconformist spirit of the person underneath the clothes. We were hooked.

Our subjects revealed the debilitating effects of marketing on our human experience. They shared stories about battles with eating disorders, drug addictions, depression, as well as gender, age and racial-identity crises. All of them had faced misguided assumptions or severe pressures all because of how they looked, including bullying and marginalization for everything from what they were wearing to the texture of their natural hair.

In 2009, we picked up a home video camera and began to document diverse people who were challenging fashion industry norms with what they wore. We wanted to get to know the people who made our heads turn when we encountered them. What made them tick and how were they able to remain true individuals in the face of a cookie cutter culture? In our 'Closet' series, we went into these people's homes and dug into their influences and ideas.

In order to dive deeper, in 2014 we launched the 'What's Underneath Project,' a series of docu-style video portraits where people of all ages, races, body types, genders and sexualities remove layers of clothing while sharing honest, empowering stories related to style, self-image and identity.

In 'What's Underneath,' the act of undressing became a powerful metaphor for shedding the binds of cultural conditioning that are placed on us all with regard to how we present ourselves to the world.

Some of our subjects were further along in liberating themselves from the scars of this societal programming, while others were just beginning. But what became so moving for us was to watch how 'What's Underneath' became a vehicle for claiming self-acceptance—for saying, 'I am okay in this moment, exactly as I am.'

We've come to understand that radical self-acceptance is the ultimate root of original personal style; a profound beauty that can be accessed inside each and every one of us.

Over the years, by giving our subjects the space to express themselves freely, each of them has in turn taught us the meaning behind true style. In this book, we've compiled their wisdom into seven chapters that we're calling our 'manifesto.' In its totality, our manifesto forges the path toward a Self-Acceptance Revolution, providing a roadmap for each of us to begin using our style as an expression of personal power and self-love, becoming part of a collective healing.

We continue to look back with amazement, reflecting on the ways in which our respective issues with the fashion industry indelibly linked us on this life-defining mission as a mother and daughter. By using our struggles as a springboard to a new course, we found ourselves, we found community, and we found hope for a more creative, loving and accepting world. It is our ultimate dream that the pages of *True Style is What's Underneath* can provide you with the same.

With so much love,
Elisa and Lily

9

tangle
le
FASHION

1.

For us, getting dressed each morning is a process of becoming our freest selves. Whatever our mood or stage of life, this daily ritual confronts us with the question: Are we thinking independently or are we buying into a status quo that undermines our individuality? By considering this, style becomes far more than a superficial aesthetic choice. Rather, style becomes an essential exploration of identity.

This self-reflection only hit us once we began to unpack the difference between fashion and style. When we started StyleLikeU, we were merely acting on a hunch that the fashion industry as we knew it had very little correlation to true personal style and the liberated beings who embody it. We needed to understand the deeper cut: What was underneath a person who possessed this brand of authentic style?

After eight years of interviews, this is what we now know: The clothes you buy—fashion—are, in their truest sense, external tools you are given to express yourself sartorially. These tools can be as simple as a white tee shirt or as extravagant as a couture gown. Style, on the other hand, comes from your spirit. It's the ease with which you move in your clothes and how that mirrors the freedom with which you live your life. It's how you interpret the tools of fashion and make them your own. If you think of your body as a blank canvas, fashion is the paint and style is what you, as an artist, create with that paint.

These days, however, through deceptive advertising, the mainstream fashion industry has grown to exploit the idea of style. With trends that are cooked up in a boardroom, we have been brainwashed into believing that there is a 'right' or 'wrong,' 'in' or 'out' way of dressing. It's prescribed. It's homogenous. It's exclusive. We have been fooled into believing that if we 'get the look' of a celebrity or snag a new head-to-toe runway look, than poof, we will magically 'have style' and maybe even belong, be happier and more fulfilled. In essence, we have been told that style is something that can be bought. This lie has distracted us from the truth that style is something that we all already possess inside.

In this chapter, we're featuring some of the gems that we have uncovered on our journey toward understanding what true personal style is. Among them are creative director Mary Randolph Carter, who resurrects the traditions of her southern roots and considers nothing too weathered or too old to be beautiful. Oblivious to rules and running 100 percent on her own whims, chef Laila Gohar's style is a moment-by-moment perfect accident, layered in humorous contradictions and reflecting her spontaneous embrace of life. Musician Jean Lebrun smashes norms as a man in a pleated skirt, calling it the height of masculinity.

Disentangle style from fashion and you can be your own archetype, deciding for yourself what feels good to you. There is no 'look' that you need but your own.

Mary Randolph Carter

CREATIVE DIRECTOR, WRITER
NEW YORK

I DON'T THINK I WAS REALLY INTO FASHION AT ALL. BUT I WAS INTO TELLING STORIES.

I'm from Richmond, Virginia, born and raised there, the oldest of nine. One of the things that was part of my life was loving the past, loving the families that brought you along, loving old things. That has stayed with me all my life. I mean, that's where it began for me.

My mom was beautiful and authentic in jeans and a sweater, but I was definitely more of a tomgirl, so I probably dress more like my father. My dad was an Atticus Finch-type who wore white shirts with chinos and loafers. With both of my parents, it wasn't about what you wore, it was how you lived.

When I moved to New York, what I loved about it was everyone was distinctive, everyone had a personality. It wasn't cookie cutter, it was anything goes.

I especially like finding vintage pieces. This is a great old riding jacket, herringbone. This coat that I just love is menswear, it's based on an old Navajo blanket. If I have to dress up black tie, I always wear a tuxedo and often I'll just throw this over the tuxedo. I love contradiction, like throwing a safari jacket over a gold beaded dress. I love old military things, I love uniforms. There's a heritage and a romance to them.

I was invited to go to the party of the year at the Met. So I put a dress on, and all of a sudden, Diana Vreeland is standing in front of me, and I'm like, aghast. And she said, 'Darling, I love your dress. Where did you get it?' Then, a little while later, I'm still recovering, and Howard [my husband] said, 'Do you realize that your dress is inside out?' Which to me, made the whole thing even better.

My hair is my biggest accessory. People say when you reach a certain age you should cut your hair. You can do whatever you want, it's fine with me, but don't tell me I can't keep my hair long if that's what makes me comfortable.

These are old Fryes. Thank God I have this great shoemaker downstairs who re-heeled and re-soled them. And he always looks at me and says, 'no polish, no polish,' and I say, 'no polish.'

It's not about things – it's about emotions: triggering memory and feeling. I'm just a person who loves to EXPLORE, HUNT AND DISCOVER.

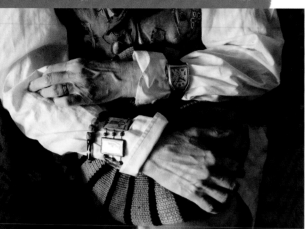

Three out of the seven days a week,
I'm in a white shirt. I think a white shirt is so
flattering. And it's just like the walls of my home,
which have always been white, because the white wall
shows off all the color and the texture.

This is an old western vest and when I first
tried it on, I looked on the back and it had the
year I was born. I always wear my watch on
top of my shirts or sweaters. I have thousands
of these little Lady of Guadalupe Mexican
bracelets. We were raised Catholic. I've always had
this love of ritual and religious items and totems.

I like who I am, I like the way I look.
There are some things that bother
me with my face, but you know what,
those are lines from my life, and
living, and I look at my beautiful
mother's face, 93 years old, she has
given birth and raised nine children,
and lost a couple along the way, and
I look at that beautiful face of hers.
I want my mother's face. My mother
and father are my bones, my heart,
everything.

I NEVER IRON
ANYTHING
I LOVE WRINKLES,
ON my FACE
and on
my Clothes.

Shirin
Neshat

I embody the clash between ideas
of traditional style and modern
westernized design. I like them both, but
I can never let go of things that remind
me of something very remote. I am
interested in things that are beautiful by
accident. Very often, say in an airport,
you'll see a not-so-wealthy Indian
woman enter, dressed so elegantly. She
is not even conscious of it, it's just how
she's used to dressing.

That is style. You don't do it
to show off, it's a way of life.

20

Myf Shepherd

I don't buy much. I will turn my house-mate's button ups into skirts. He will say, 'Where's my denim shirt?' and I say, 'You mean my skirt?'

I change my outfit only slightly from one day to the next, so it's an evolution.

Larkin Grimm

Personal style is an externalization of the soul.

Shantell Martin

**ARTIST
NEW YORK**

I've always worn what I've been comfortable with. Naturally, over the years, this has become my style.

I've been wearing the same thing since I was kid—a tee shirt, with either jeans or shorts. Coming from a family that didn't have that much money, there was always the pressure of trying to have things that other people have, but, at the end of the day, I didn't care.

This is my attempt at dressing up—just a white shirt from Uniqlo that I drew on spontaneously and these super soft Levi's jeans that got paint and stuff on them from what I've been working on.

If I dress up, it feels weird, like I'm in some strange uniform trying to be someone else from another planet. It doesn't feel right.

I have four blond sisters and a blond brother (we have a different dad). Growing up in a very white working class environment, and being brown with an afro already put me on the outside of everything else that was going on. When you do not look like everyone else there is this kind of natural seclusion.

So I was able to do my own thing and not have any pressure to fit in. I think that really helped me be comfortable with being different and be very confident being myself.

I like to draw on my shoes. I have some questions on them like 'Do You Read?' Art should be inclusive: a two-way connection between you and the viewer. I just did a show and there was a plumber working on the building. He came up to me at the end and he said, 'I'm your biggest fan and I'm going to bring my wife in if that's okay.'

I like the feeling of white, unknown space that you can add to. With black and white, there's so much room for discovery.

When the plumber walks in off the street and says he loves your show, then you know you're doing something right.

If you have good intention behind what you're drawing, then what you're thinking about and what you're going through comes out. I like to think about everything as one big mistake.

I have no aspirations to sanity whatsoever. When I look around and see what is considered normal, I am not tempted.

Timothy John

Style is all about expressing your individuality freely and courageously. But we're living in an age of fear. Not many people make decisions based on joy.

Fred
Butler

My style
is really
weird
so I
think
it's difficult to get your head
around that it might be tasteful.

Laila Gohar

FOOD DESIGNER
NEW YORK

I'm not really into trends. I think they are for people who can't be bothered to come up with their own ideas.

I am from Egypt. Growing up in Cairo, the society is very contained, you're held to certain ideals and you're meant to look a certain way and act a certain way. However, my sister and I were encouraged to dress how we wanted and express ourselves as we wanted. When I'm walking down the street and more conservative people give me disapproving looks—I love it. I find it really fascinating to interact with people through what I'm wearing, even if it's a silent interaction.

When I wake up every Morning and get dressed, I can become WHATEVER Character that I want.

I feel that the happier I am, the more flamboyant I am in the way that I dress and in the food that I eat. I think for me the two go hand in hand. My mood is definitely reflective of what I put inside my body and out.
Food is what you nourish your soul and body with, clothes are what you put on the outside.

28

These are just my zebra shoes. I think they kind of make my feet look big, like a man. For me, it's important to have a sense of humor.

These overalls are U.S. Army, Navy . . . one of, you know, the fighters. Kids get very excited about these sneakers, which I really enjoy. They have these little wings on them. I like how you never would imagine these overalls with these shoes.

This shawl is just a piece of fabric from Morocco. I had a full-fledged obsession with Morocco. I am very obsessive when it comes to everything in life.

Indigenous communities have been repressed and oppressed, but they still manage to express so much of themselves. When you have very little, in the end you can produce something so grand. When you have a lot, you sort of become nearsighted.

I hate the look of someone who looks like they just pranced off the runway. I think that's the worst.

29

This is a Thai warrior coat from the eighteenth century, or at least that's what the guy from the auction house told me. The person I bought it from asked me what I was going to do with it, and whether I was going to hang it on the wall, and I told him of course not, that I would wear it.

This is a hood. I wear it on days when I want to be in my own little bubble. I've realized, though, that it kind of defeats the purpose because it does attract people's attention. When I was young there was a boy in an Egyptian movie who would wear a hat to become invisible. I used to tell my mom that I wanted to be invisible. My mom would say, 'No one should want to be invisible. You should want to show yourself to the world.'

I hope to always have the imagination of a child, so this is the closest I've come to the invisible hat.

Jimmy Webb

You know what style is? Truth and energy. Iggy Pop's the most stylish person in the world I know, and he's naked all the time. That is style.

Style is the RAW POWER of the TRUTH.

I don't see things in boxes. My style is my own curation of what I'm feeling in my body and in my life and it's continuously evolving. It's my chance to enact a narrative on a daily basis even if everything around me feels completely stale.

Minka Sicklinger

Louise Sturges

Every single person wakes up and makes a decision about how the world will see them. I tend to push it. It is disarming and exciting.

I don't take how I dress too seriously— you have to have a sense of humor.

Henny Garfunkel

PHOTOGRAPHER
NEW YORK

I love clowning. I want people to look at me and think, 'What the fuck?' People are afraid they're not going to fit in—they want to be beige. 'The Gapification,' I call it.

I believe that high heels are something on par with when the Chinese used to bind women's feet. People think they make your legs look great but they bind your mind and bind your body—you can't run away from a rapist, that's for sure. You are on this pedestal and you look good but you can't move, so you need to be carried. As a woman, you should be able to be on the move.

Beauty is visceral, you can't put your finger on it, but you know it when you see it. It is a Nepalese or Tibetan woman who is in full regalia. I think it comes back to strength.

Giovanni James

ARTIST
NEW YORK

My clothes may be stylish to other people, but they are not to me. I like a refined, mangled look. I like the coming together of different worlds. If something is nice, I will destroy it organically so that it has a story and a history to it. It makes it much richer.

I've always been deeply in love with anything that was cool, whether it came from my Caucasian or African-American side. I would mix prep with street and rock L.L. Bean in the hood and a nameplate belt buckle in suburbia. As a kid, I was the ambassador between the hood and suburbia.

I've been on my own since I was 13. I was homeless. With time and experience I have come to see the many blessings of that. I got to live with different families and their cultures. I realized that these different groups—Jews, Catholics, Blacks, Whites—were pretty cool and I got to examine them all. I didn't have a specific dogma put on me. I literally have been a vessel, able to experience other people's lives, and it has left me, in moments, identity-less and open to humanity. What I found is that being here is such a gift. Let's do something, make something beautiful aside from just making money. We can't take that with us.

I am into the style of NO STYLE.
→→→

I love 'fuck it' pants. 'Fuck it' pants are pants you don't have to think about. You can wipe your hands on them, you can be a child. It's like wearing a bib. They feel like art to me, like a canvas because of the life they've lived.

What inspires me about past eras is that things weren't made to be consumed and then thrown away, they were made to last.

So I find myself attracted to older things with a deeper message. Clothes now are made from the standpoint of consumers using them, then destroying them, and then buying more.

I don't think real beauty can be articulated, it's a feeling. I think life is beautiful and people are blind to it. We're so wrapped up in these narratives and stories and it's like we're functioning schizophrenics. We're also beings of exploitation. In the system we live in, we're all exploiting somebody to get to another place. So if you don't make people crazy and delusional, then this system fails.

I feel that one of my missions in life as an artist is to show us all the possibilities of who we are.

Agathe Snow

I don't really buy clothes, I make things with what I have around. A lot of people give me their things, it's like a community.

That's my expression, living in this little world I have made for myself. I want to be able to keep evolving, to keep moving, to keep changing and to shed.

Gloria
Baume

To me, fashion is a Call of the Wild.

Jean Lebrun

ARTIST, MUSICIAN
LOS ANGELES

I look at STYLE
AS AN ART form.
It's a RITUAL.
My style says that
I'm a Free Person

My mom was super religious and as a child I couldn't be as free as I am now. Today I'm able to capture that freedom. People assume all cool things when they see me. Even if they don't fully understand it, they see something they maybe haven't been exposed to . . . it's contagious.

I'm FREE, I can wear whatever I want and still be A Fucking Man.

I'm a fan of pleated skirts, they remind me of schoolgirl uniforms from when I went to a Catholic school in the first and second grade. I also gravitate to royal blue. I vibe off the energy. It flows well with my skin, it makes me feel light. It's like electricity, water, and the sky. And then mixing it all with a basketball jersey—the feeling of being in the park with my homies to play basketball, in some sweats, just being super comfortable.

It's funny that people would attach the way you dress to being gay. Where I am from, the people are so close-minded. We grew up listening to Onyx and DMX and Wu-Tang Clan, and when they see Marilyn Manson, Iggy Pop, Alice Cooper, they're like, 'No, not for me,' just don't even give it a try. For me, when I see someone so radical, I think whoa . . . the fact that you had the balls to do that—that inspires me. Where I come from, the gay dudes are very flamboyant, that's inspiring too. Like they don't give a fuck. That shit is mad dope to me.

42

Obviously, when people see you in a skirt, or they see lipstick, or certain things, they're like, 'aw man, he's gotta be gay.'

I can't find too many hats that fit my hair, so this leopard hat works magic. I get compliments from really old ladies, they love my hats. It's a beautiful thing.

Here on my fingers it says 'Love Life.' I love life. Every day I wake up in the morning and I definitely praise; I give thanks to being alive. I have faith in a higher power. I believe it's within us. Once you find yourself, then everything else flows. ⇢⟫⟫•—⇢

When I wear all white that's my ghost look. When I'm ghosting, they can't stop me, I am smokes and fumes, appearing and disappearing, moving in different shapes. The handcuffs are a reflection of

the hood, getting locked up by the cops for dumb shit. When I'm wearing this belt, I feel like I'm authority.

The music I'm making now is very aggressive, defaced, mysterious, and fun, reflecting where I'm at today in my style. We've struggled and actually tried really hard for success with our music, so, we want you to feel it. You feel our pain. I gotta fucking work hard, because my mom is still working hard. My friends back home aren't where they need to be. I've got obligations.

Robert Richards

I hate red carpet commotion. Nobody takes a chance. Corporate beauty is cheap and available to everybody. If you're eccentric, you can make the dullest thing totally crazy.

Jasmine Croissant

I don't change what I'm wearing for anything that I'm doing. I ride my bike everywhere in the city in short skirts or high heels or a crazy wedding outfit. I like crossing boundaries of something not having a function but looking alive and fresh and wild. Some of my best days are when I don't give two fucks what I look like.

Erin O'Connor

I was on a job once and the hairdresser said, 'If you want to get ahead in the industry, get your boobs done.' Something interesting happened from that day forward for me. I have not always been kind to myself in terms of how much I love my body and my image, but when somebody else dared to attack me, that was it. A light went on, and I knew that I would never change my appearance.

Mattie Barringer

I'm becoming the person I want to be, not the person in the magazine.

Rashida Robinson

I love a good uniform because you don't have to think about what you put on. It's the freedom to be able to be comfortable and still looked dressed up.

Michèle Lamy

My ancestors are from North Africa, they're Berbers. I believe genes have memory. I love painting my face, I wake up in the morning and do it with a crayon. My head doesn't function without it. Snoop Dogg is my idol. All these years, he has been right style-wise. I like his attitude.

I have a good nature, so I always find something beautiful. I follow a flow of attraction.

Miguel
Adrover

DESIGNER
MALLORCA

It's not about fashion, it's about the balls you have to wear what you wear and to express yourself.

I've always been attracted to different societies, different cultures, and different ways of dressing. I never saw it as fashion. For me, fashion is all of that couture in Paris — it is something high class. I am much more into social and environmental movements.

I love costumes, and I don't see any taboos in costumes. I wear a skirt if I want to wear a skirt, I wear makeup if I want to wear makeup, I wear heels if I want to wear heels. People take it as a superficial thing, but a lot of people around the world still get killed, beaten up, and raped for the way they dress.

My second collection was all fabrics I found in the garbage. 'Dirty' was a theme because Giuliani was the mayor then. He closed all the shelters on the Bowery and everybody was really upset about it. I mixed dirty clothes with clean clothes, because I wanted to make dirty look beautiful. There was a Burberry raincoat, inside out and backwards. We called it Midtown because it was a mixture of people from Uptown and Downtown — they met in the middle.

People kill for Louis Vuitton bags. How disgusting to pay thousands of dollars on a bag and in six months throw it away and get another one. It's so impersonal. People desire to consume so they can show off for other people. You're only happy for a second, because some friend is saying that you don't have the newest bag.

Trends are empty. They question nothing. Nobody asks why this week we're wearing bell bottom pants and next week we're wearing skinny jeans. It's people who don't have their own personality who have the need to change with the trends.

For me, it takes a long time to feel comfortable in a certain hat and to walk down the street with that hat and feel it as a part of myself. I don't consider that a trend. I consider it a piece of clothing that I like to wear and combine with other clothes. What I have, I can live out my life with. I can develop millions of styles. But trends are just marketing to sell more clothes, they're not necessary. They're like snacks — after you eat them, your stomach is still empty. You need the real meal. And, today, it's hard to find a real meal.

I don't believe in God. I believe in good. The goals of our society don't really help you to do good. These days, I see a long highway with a big sign at the end of the road that says: Fame, money, glamour, beauty, power. I see thousands of cars going fast to catch that road. You see people dead on the sidewalk.

My road has no sign on the end. You just need to live every step. How else are we going to sustain this planet? Clothes are not a big deal. 'It's just clothes,' Lee [Alexander] McQueen used to say, and he was right. Clothes are powerful but if you take them out of the system of fashion they're more powerful.

Clothes are powerful but if you take them out of the system of fashion they're more powerful.

When fashion tied itself to POWER, it become married to the DEVIL. Capitalism is on steroids.

Dre
Expres
Inner

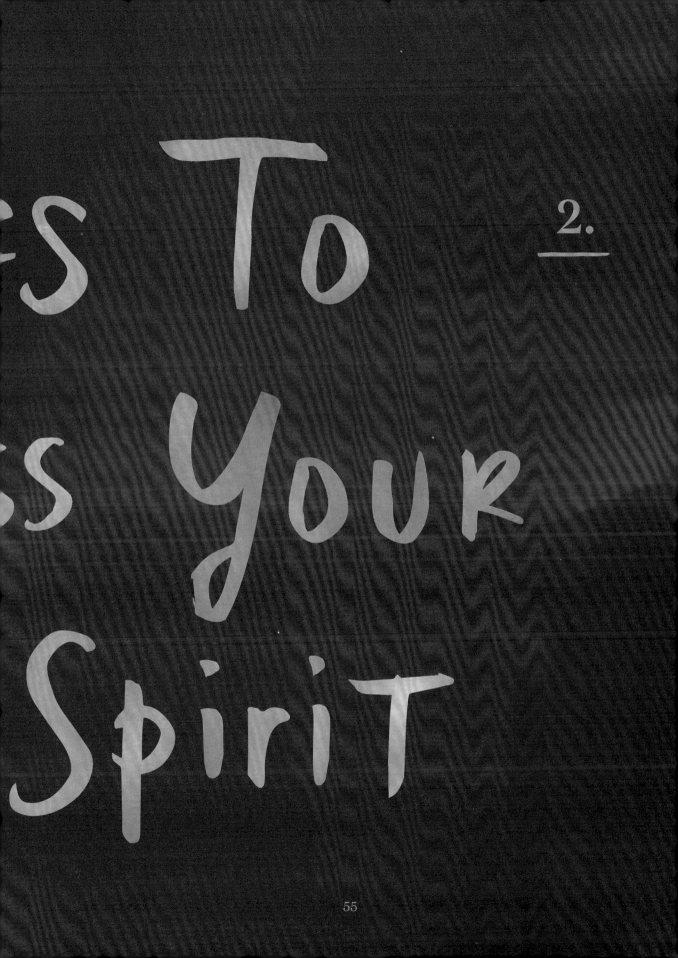

When I, Lily, was a teenager, I was a victim of the fashion industry's brainwashing. I believed that style meant looking like the industry's ordained "IT" girls of the day: Kate Moss, Sienna Miller, and Mary-Kate Olsen. These were girls with whom I shared very little in common, looks and otherwise. They were waifey and I was voluptuous. They were rebellious and cool, and I was an overachieving nerd.

On a tortuous quest to emulate them, I spent years starving myself so that I could eventually squeeze my curves into skinny jeans. Shopping for said jeans, without fail, ended with me in tears, as my love handles spilled over even the largest size. In this mode of being, I was a slave to someone else's ideal of how I should look, denying who I was in order to fit in, rather than discovering what was true to me. This mentality turned style into something narrow and unattainable, something that felt unavailable to me simply because of who I was.

When I started StyleLikeU, everything changed. The diverse and unpretentious people I was interviewing, and the community of alternative thinkers I was bringing together, woke me up to the idea that true style is something much more personal, empowering, and creative than I had ever known. I realized that getting dressed every morning was an opportunity to communicate something about who I was.

When this finally dawned on me, putting clothes together was no longer an oppressive experience. Instead, it began to be a soulful one, becoming an expression of my emerging self-acceptance. I was ready to be real, inspired, and free, and I became in touch with clothing that reflected that energy. Dresses became my jeans-and-tee-shirt, and colors, embroidery, and prints became my neutrals. My mom began to encourage me to keep my closet door open because she felt that it was becoming art: my essence in clothing form.

So, next time you're in your closet, look at what's there and ask yourself: Did I buy these things because they spoke to me for a deeply personal reason or did I buy them to fit into fashion's fabricated idea of 'cool?'

As musician Annakim Violette says in this chapter, 'Clothing shouldn't be about trying to fit into or out of the world.' Instead of feeling like you need to suppress yourself in order to have style, get in touch with what inspires you and use your imagination. Once you do that, getting dressed will no longer break your spirit, but may actually set you free.

Tatiana
Pajkovic

**ACTRESS, MUSICIAN, MODEL
BROOKLYN**

I love to take something that's ugly and make it shine.

I'm wearing boxing shorts because I love things that have to do with boxing. I love to pair them with something super feminine, like this ugly purple nylon jacket that I found in a vintage shop.

I'm from Copenhagen. I was brought up with a lot of guys. I had this 'No, I want to swim the fastest! I want the guys to think I'm cool' way of thinking. Now, in my adult life, the masculine-feminine labels aren't important to me. As long as you're true to your instincts, you're super cool. I'm fascinated when people are totally themselves. I don't mind if people are inappropriate or have bad manners, as long as it's who they are, it's fine.

My definition of beauty is something that you can't see with your eyes. It's something you feel and express from a place that doesn't have any beauty. I love to take something that's ugly and make it shine.

Dressing creatively makes me as happy as when my favorite song is playing super loud in the car. I feel like I've won the lottery when I find something that's 'The Thing.' If something is kooky enough that I think I can make it work, then I can't wait to take it home and do it justice.

When I look back on the months when I had only 30 dollars and had to eat tuna fish every day in a cockroach-filled apartment, I think: Fuck ... my thoughts were so much simpler then. I felt like everything sucked, but I used that energy to produce. It's important to have an energy and to be enthusiastic about every day and every thing—even if at the moment it all just seems like the worst thing.

I'm wearing a Dior night-gown. It's like this hip grandma nightgown that I'll wear out with a vintage rockstar hat and Adidas sneaks.

I promised myself never to be scared to wear anything. I want to look back and think: "Did I really wear that?"

›››⟩◇

This is a Thelma and Louise outfit. I got these red leather pants because I thought they were the ugliest thing I'd ever seen. I love to go against the rules I was taught when I was little, like how you aren't supposed to wear two different shades of red. So I thought it would be fun to take a bunch of red pieces in different tones and put them together.

Mara Hruby

**SINGER, SONGWRITER
OAKLAND**

I'm from Oakland, California, born and raised. My mother was a flight attendant—Bohemian-Czech. And my father was a pilot, very mixed, African-American, German, Creole, and Cherokee. Our family was built around the stories my parents brought back from traveling around the world. They taught me to believe in culture and beauty and to go beyond what directly surrounds us.

My parents didn't want me to focus on race, but to understand that everyone is equal.

Growing up, everything we did had a soundtrack. When we sat down to eat dinner, music was playing. Billie Holiday was one of my favorites. Kids would ask me what I was listening to and laugh at me because it wasn't popular stuff on the radio.

I was really into movies from the '30s, '40, '50s, '60s. Rita Hayworth, Ginger Rogers—I would pay attention to their manners, the language they used, and the dispositions of the women compared to the men. I enjoyed the elegance, the class, and the grace that the women of the time carried.

I've been through a lot of darkness,

but when I wear vintage I can carry myself like it doesn't matter.

63

Nadia Sarwar

I'm inspired by theories and moods more than people. I like the personality of America in the '90s.

Elijah Pryor

My style is my get-away. It's my island where I fly to when everything seems out of place. It is my door that opens up and takes me to my dreams.

Bonnie Young

I love being absorbed in different cultures. It's not really about where you're from. Cultural rituals are inspirational because they're effortless. With the Szechuan tribes, the combination of the jewelry, the color, and the fabric looks like a movie set. Then you go to the monasteries and see monks and their red robes perfectly draped against washed walls. You couldn't script it.

I feel more in common with someone
from the Middle East than I do with
someone I grew up with in New York.

Aymeric Bergada du Cadet

ART DIRECTOR
PARIS

I'm not comfortable in comfortable clothes.

I can't live in white walls. I call it Gone with the Wind Syndrome. There's a scene in the movie where Scarlett goes to visit Rhett in jail and she doesn't want him to see her in her old plain outfit, so she takes down the velvet curtains and makes a dress with them. I love that: Make a dress out of curtains and go out.

I need to feel the personality of things. Not a lot of people decorate their place this way. For them, it's un-useful to have fabric collecting dust.

I think that MORE is the New Black.

When it's considered un-useful, it excites me. I was a very shy child, even if you can't believe it when you see me.

When you're really shy and in a room full of fabulous people and too scared to say anything, your clothes can say it for you.

I don't love shopping, but searching for old pieces, rare stuff, is like hunting. I wear many layers, so I can't move my arms much, but it keeps me sitting still and straight. I'm not comfortable in comfortable clothes.

When I style people, the moment I like best is when we put on the base, like the stockings and then the heels, and then it's always crazy because you see everything change. Not just the clothes, but everything. The body changes, the attitude changes. I love the moment when someone who is not used to having complicated clothes on suddenly sees themselves in the mirror and realizes that with clothing they can be whomever they aspire to be.

This is something I do a lot, combining woman's tights or suspenders with colored tights. I have a big thing for stockings.

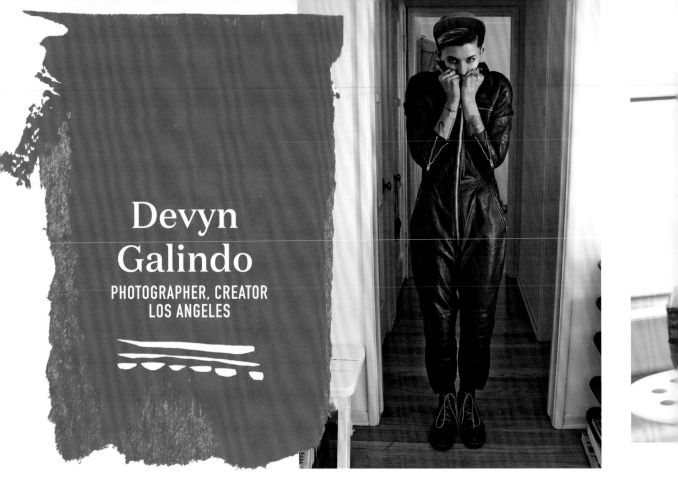

Devyn Galindo

**PHOTOGRAPHER, CREATOR
LOS ANGELES**

My stepdad was a foreman and I would see him wear Carhartt jumpsuits and uniforms. Now I wear those things to represent the beauty in everyday life, like people sweeping wearing this beautiful bright blue.

'I'm not frightened by anyone's perception of me.' That was my first tattoo. I got it when I was 18 and I was finally okay with just being 100 percent me. I felt: No one is ever going to tell me who I am. Most of my tattoos—'Stay Humble,' 'Humble Me'—are daily reminders of where I come from (or the 500 places I come from).

I'm influenced by blue collar workwear.

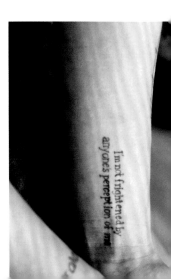

70

I love incorporating the beauty of everyday life into my own personal style.

People stare at me all the time. I think of it as a social experiment. I'll be walking down the street and they'll stop for a second glance. They'll say, 'Sir . . . I mean ma'am . . .' It means that I'm representing all of the ideas. Floating between worlds is important to me.

71

Guy Blakeslee

This jacket, around town people say, 'It's that guy again! The polka dot dude!' Because I always wear it and it seems to elicit a jolly response from people. I like to walk into a room and have people smile at me because it's not comical, it's jester-like.

Amanda Charchian

Sunday best is all the time. I've never felt comfortable in jeans and sweatpants.

People used to dress up when they went to protests, and that always really resonated with me.

I want my clothing to spark an interaction with people.

Thaddeus O'Neill

I try to keep my clothing open to accident and I try to keep it poetic—having the rhythm and structure of a Rimbaud or Walt Whitman poem.

Sometimes I'm shy or timid. My clothing is a way to offset that shyness. I'm not a loud person, so it's my way of being a little louder.

Shirley
Kurata

Terry
Lovette

I was
taught
to be
spiritually
strong and I exude that in
the way that I dress.

Carolyn Roumeguere

JEWELRY AND INTERIOR DESIGNER
GERMANTOWN AND KENYA

My wardrobe is full of things that are made by friends or from faraway places, so everything's special.

I only shop vintage, or get things from my friends who are designers. We do trades. Or I have things made in Peru or Kenya or wherever I'm traveling. My style is about the people I love. I'll put on an Alice Temperley gown, which people wear on the red carpet, with my biker boots. I'll wear it to a Sunday brunch. I don't wait for a special occasion to wear a long beautiful dress, because it makes me feel good.

My mother fell in love with the Maasai culture on a trip to Kenya in the mid-sixties and that's how I ended up with the Maasai. She married a Maasai warrior who brought me and my brother and sister up. He later married another eight wives. Thanks to my connection with the Maasai and thanks to being brought up with them, there were always women making jewelry, so I would make it with them. I started with beads, always handmade, always working with people in remote places who knew their craft.

I bought this orange beaded neck piece from a warrior at the border between Kenya and Tanzania, near Kilimanjaro. Maybe it's the energy of the warrior who sold it to me that I love. Orange is also one of my favorite colors, it's the color of fire and feeling.

This is from a sari of organza silk that I had made into a top. I think the sari is one of the most elegant forms of clothing. I love the fabric—you can wear it, you can put it on the bed, you can take it on a picnic, you can hang it on a wall, it adds beautiful energy and immediately transforms the space. I actually have a couple of pieces of fabric that I travel with, that go everywhere with me,

There's always a feather, I have to have a feather, whether it's in my hair or in my ear. It symbolizes freedom, the flight of an eagle, seeing life from a broader perspective. Think big and you feel the whole world, wherever you are. I've always loved rocks as well and being connected to the earth.

I was born in Paris and went to Africa when I was nine months old. My mother made a bridge between the two worlds, because among the Maasai, I'm considered one of them. I speak the language and I can totally relate to that culture, and yet I can also relate to anyone in Paris, London, or New York. And more importantly, they can relate to me. There's such a craving for tradition in the Western world, a looking back, thinking, how did we get here and how do we get back to something more like what we used to be?

I was lucky to grow up with the Maasai and these warriors, I was around fearless people and it had a great impact on me. Also, the Maasai are very fluid, they're nomads, they carry whatever they can on the back of a donkey. I once saw one of them throw away

a brand new radio, and my mother said to him, 'Is it not working?' and he said, 'Oh no, it works fine, but there's no room on the donkey for that.' There's no attachment to material things.

My friends are shocked that I will sell a piece of mine that I really love. Who we are is inside and not physical and does not have a price tag on it.

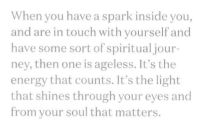

I think in our society it would be good to get back to rituals, and to ceremonies. We have funerals and birthdays and that's about it, but in traditional societies, there's a lot more. They instill in everyone, even children, a sense of reverence for the harvest and rain. We've lost our sense of community, of living in a small village and we need it. We're not made to live in a little corner all by ourselves; This is why everyone needs to go talk to a therapist. In a community, there are the elders, you have someone to talk to. You get the support.

When you have a spark inside you, and are in touch with yourself and have some sort of spiritual journey, then one is ageless. It's the energy that counts. It's the light that shines through your eyes and from your soul that matters.

With age people become who they're meant to become. I feel more beautiful than ever.

Lia Chavez

My grandmother Doris is one of my great inspirations. When she married my Mexican grandfather, her German father disowned her. His parting words to her were, 'Your children will never have any shoes.' She took that and turned it into fuel. She would have a pair of shoes in every color, so her closet was a rainbow. She was considered the one with 'bad taste,' which actually really means awesome, individual style.

SoKo

I sway sexually between everything. I love men and women and animals (in a friendly way). I feel like we're not just one thing and I would get really bored if I was given the option to only wear one type of clothes for the rest of my life. I like switching it up and looking very girly one day and dressing like a man the next.

Scarlett Rouge

People are going to judge you or have some sort of assumptions about you the first second they see you. And really, persona is a mask and the way you dress is also part of that mask.

I was raised by cross-dressers, so I feel very connected to that over-the-top decadence.

Leah Hennessey

**WRITER, MUSICIAN, ACTRESS
NEW YORK**

I don't think there is anything unique or one of a kind about any aspect of my style, and I'm proud to say that I'm a magpie. It's tribal in that I dress like the people who I belong to. I think it's so funny when people get upset—and I'm guilty of this too— about their friends ripping off their style. You can try to have boundaries but when you love someone enough, then it just kind of seeps into you by osmosis and you start making it part of who you are.

My style reveals the people that I love and emulate

I made this striped tee shirt dress last summer. I was inspired by a picture of Veruschka on the beach in the '60s, and I thought, I want something that makes me feel like that. Last summer I wore it every day, and this summer my friends asked, 'Where's that orange dress you have? You were like Charlie Brown! You had one look.'

I think accepting who you are in the shadows of those you admire and seeing the difference, and being able to live with the difference, is the beginning of self-acceptance.

The difference be-tween what you aim to be and what you are in the moment, that's actually what you are.

For example, every girl in my world at one point wanted to look like David Bowie. But you look in the mirror—you don't have that body, you don't have fucked-up teeth, you're not starving to death and surviving on cocaine. That's not who I am; I'm me. But that doesn't mean I can't still try to look like David Bowie.

There's a perversity that makes people feel like it's sinful to be indulgent and true to your impulses. It's okay to be a little reckless with your appearance and to be creative about it— you're not as attached that way. Some people will freak out over a weird hair day and go into a shame spiral. People need to be willing to give up on their ideas of who they think they are so that they can question what they have been told.

People need to be willing to give up on their ideas of who they think they are.

C. Madeleine

There is not a question in my mind that when you lose a sense, the other senses become much greater. My visual is an explosion of color, and if not for the trials of being deaf, I wouldn't be the person that I am today. I wouldn't be Madeleine.

Preston Smiles

Everything I saw in high school said that young African-American men were not supposed to be smart. They were supposed to dress, talk, and be a certain way. I started believing that, so I decided to be in a gang with my friends. One day, my friends came over and we were about to do the same thing we did every day: Get some alcohol, smoke weed, and be dumb kids. But that day, something in me was like 'STAY.' Within a couple of hours, every person in that car was shot. I stepped out of wanting to be a badass and moved more into my artistic side, and I started expressing myself through my clothes.

Scout Willis

When I wake up, I dress exactly how I'm feeling that day, depending on what music I'm listening to and what movie I've just watched. I like creating little narratives for myself, like if I need to be a really strong female persona that day. It's not becoming other people, but bringing out different sides of me.

As long as you are trying to dress like someone else or be someone else you will always be second best.

87

Annakim Violette

**VAMPIRE
LOS ANGELES**

Clothing shouldn't be about trying to fit into or out of the world.

We've been taught to think in a consumer way. We're in a culture where everyone's born a drug addict whether they're taking drugs or not. We're in an addictive culture. I feel like the only way I can really relate to people is to get past all the labels.

I made a deal with the devil not to eat much for a couple of months just to get this dress.

There's something so vivid about a rainbow because its beauty has had to come from insane storm clouds.

We need to step back and ask ourselves: What does this make me feel? For example, I got this dress because I think it's interesting that I'm still living in a gun country. The hatred in the world inspires me because I feel like it comes from the same place as love. Pain and joy — they're not different to me. You can be scared or euphorically happy. It feels like an almost identical place. My eyes, whenever I laugh, always seem to cry too.

Anyone else's closet makes my heart beat like a Japanese horror movie. I think: How did they get to the point where they have all of this stuff? It's interesting to see how people view their strengths and their weaknesses through their armor.

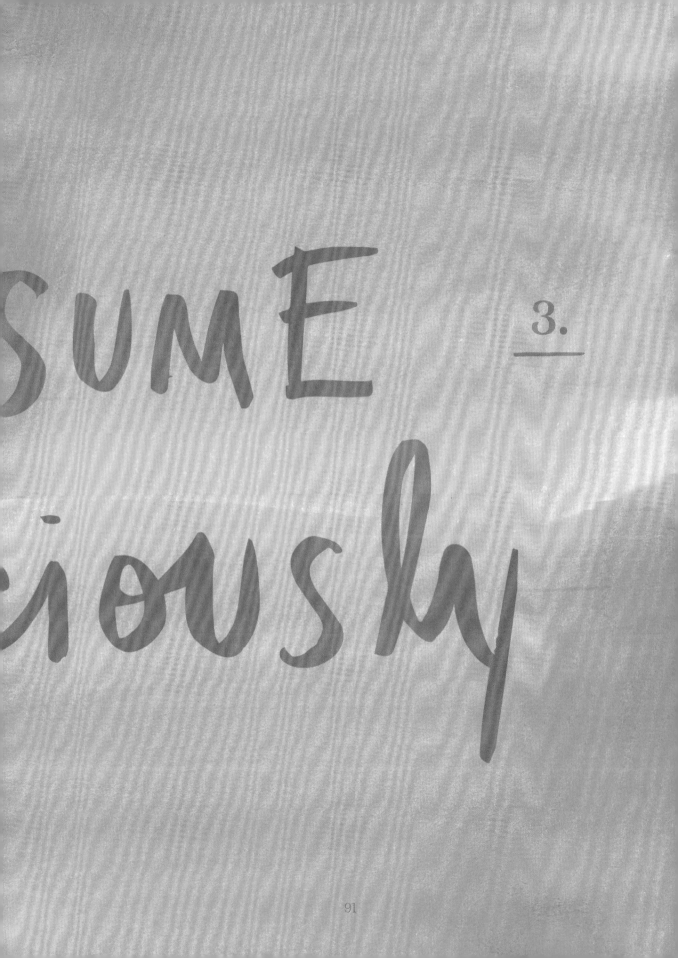

SUmE

ciously

Since starting StyleLikeU, there has not been one person we have interviewed who consumes blindly. Each, in their own way, consumes with intent. This has lead us to draw the inherent connection between style and consciousness, which can mean different things to different people—it is not necessarily about going green.

For some people that we've interviewed, consciousness is a commitment to understanding where their clothing comes from. For others, it's a stringent awareness of the media that they consume and how it affects their self-image. Some use their consciousness to make a rebellious statement and some use it to uphold tradition, depending on what matters to them. But regardless of how they approach it, authentic personal style is a mindful act.

In this chapter, for instance, we look at Leslie Crow, a designer who lives off the grid in a log cabin in rural Texas. One of the primary tenets of her style is exemplifying a more environmentally responsible way of life. This can mean exclusively using hides of humanely treated animals for her leather accessory business, or it can mean wearing much of the same clothing she has worn since high school. In the same way that Leslie uses her clothes to make a statement on sustainability, Wamuhu Waweru is dedicated to making sure any money she spends on clothes goes directly back to local communities in Africa like the one she comes from in Kenya. By refusing mass-manufactured products, she is using the power of her dollar to preserve local cultures for future generations.

For me, Elisa, I never spend money on anything that I'll only wear once and I rarely throw anything out. Each thing is my 'favorite' piece. This enables me to transform my outfits—multi-layered confections of items I've collected over decades—into an usual creation that embodies my (very) emotional inner world. Layering disparate items on top of one another is my joyful way of exhibiting my dissent against conformity without words. Over the years, style has become a walking, living language that lets me be seen as exactly who I am, a questioning mind who needs to expand and push boundaries.

For me, Lily, consuming consciously is an active unlearning. I purposefully follow women on social media who embrace their curves, which emboldens me to do the same. In my style, I am committed to purchasing items—such as cropped tops, high-waisted skirts, and hip-hugging dresses—that reveal parts of my figure, like my hips and arms, that were once sources of shame, but are now tethered to my pride.

We can't define consciousness for you, but what we do know is that an element of intent is intrinsic to style. We vote with our money and brainpower, so whether you are aware of it or not, you are making a political statement with what you wear and what you look at. So, instead of asking yourself whether you're maintaining relevance, try asking yourself, what issues are relevant to me?

Arpana Rayamajhi

ARTIST, JEWELRY DESIGNER
NEW YORK

I'm always looking for objects that I feel are going to have value regardless of what trends might be.

I've been beading since I was a child. My mom and I would make really simple beaded necklaces, it's part of Nepali women's culture. Now I use Nepali coins in the necklaces I make. It's a way for me to incorporate a craft form that is universal, and then take it to somewhere specific, hence the coins.

I'm from Nepal and I live in New York and I have been very fortunate to be able to travel to different parts of the world, which has made me understand people and cultures. It's shown me differences, but it's also shown me similarities, which seem much stronger than the differences. There are symbols, patterns, textiles, and ideas that are universal.

To think that you can only wear an object if you are part of that culture feels actually really exclusive and divisive to me. I'm not defending the irresponsibility of the big corporations. But how can you say to an autonomous person that they have no right to wear what they want, to look the way they want?

In Nepal, if you, as a foreigner, come to visit and want to eat our food that we eat every day, or if you want to wear our clothes, or if you make an attempt to speak our language, no matter how ridiculous your accent might sound, we might laugh but we find it endearing. We like it and actually want you to be a part of our culture; we think that's respectful.

The Nepalese wear beads specifically as a signifier of weddings and being married as a woman. When you are widowed, you stop wearing these beads. I thought the beads were some of the most beautiful things ever, but I was technically not allowed to wear them. I defied those norms while growing up because I felt like an object can have a life of its own, irrespective of what meanings others attach to it.

I wear things that I love, things that I gravitate towards, it becomes a repetitive pattern. People generally think I am a hippie and do psychedelic drugs because I wear a lot of colors and patterns, have long hair . . . and I guess maybe because I'm brown?

I think something is really beautiful when it's at peace with itself.

I wear beautiful dresses that I bought from southern Mexico. It doesn't make me understand their culture, it doesn't make me understand the people, it doesn't make me understand their history. But what it does make me understand is that we as humans around the world value certain things in life, that we have a collective consciousness.

The pajama suit I bought in a store near my house, which kind of weirdly serves as a little quirky toy store meets vintage meets costume meets anything wacky. If I look at the patterns and the way the drawings and illustrations look, I realize I have seen similar styles of pattern-making in India and in North Africa.

Colombia has some of the most beautiful beadwork. I read a lot on the history of beads and I was super fascinated to understand how it was one of the first forms of trading between humans. Essentially, the trading of beads could have also helped the development of language.

I have a very interesting relationship with clothes. I'm aware that adornment is superficial and we don't need it, but at the same time I feel like if clothing is superficial, the fact that we want to see good films is also superficial, as is good art, or good music. Ultimately, do any of these things really matter? No. But, they kind of do. It's a language and when I wear these pieces I feel a psychic connection, as with art.

Ferrari
Sheppard

I think our culture has deeply embedded Messiah complexes;

the ingrained, indoctrinated religion that you'll always have a savior and everything will be okay if you just look outside yourself to some bigger being, which is the celebrity, the politician, the pope. Instead of looking at yourself and saying maybe, on some small level, I am that change.

I believe that a dollar is a vote

If, as a female musician, you want to reach the highest level of commercial success, it helps if you don't have strong feelings about endorsing a particular brand whose manufacturing and labor laws suck, or a brand who has a history of racism in their advertising. It's helpful if you just don't think about that stuff, but I can't help but think about that stuff.

Samantha
Urbani

Yuna

I started wearing the hijab when I was 19 years old. Being Muslim, you're supposed to cover up. You have to be modest in life, and that is something that I relate to.

Sarah Ellison

The digital age has made it so easy to learn exactly what sells, what the general public likes and doesn't like, and how people will react to anything. When those things weren't so easily trackable, there was a mystery to it, which left room for mistakes. Some weird thing would magically do really well and nobody knew why. Now everything is so perfectly tracked that they keep feeding people more of what they already buy. Nobody wants to take a risk. Everybody is a slave to the 'like' button. We've created a zombie nation.

Hilary Walsh

I've had this shirt since high school. I've probably worn it once a week my whole life.

Sarah Sophie Flicker

CREATIVE DIRECTOR, MOVEMENT BUILDER
BROOKLYN

I don't ever wear anything that makes me look like I might be a republican.

I want to make it clear where I stand politically.

I grew up in Copenhagen where my earliest memories are of jazz clubs. My parents met in a jazz club. My dad saw my mom from across a smoky room and said, 'That's the woman I'm going to marry.' When I was four, I dreamt that Dorothy's ruby slippers were in my closet. When I woke up, they weren't, so I felt this shattering disappointment.

we look at our past to understand our present and try to make a better future.

The anarchist activist Emma Goldman said, to paraphrase: 'I don't want the revolution if I can't dance.' Those ideas have always stuck with me—activism and politics and changing paradigms also have to be fun.

I think it's our job when we exist in places of privilege to call out injustice when we see it. The onus is on me to help dispel or equalize the playing field in places that might be equal for me but aren't for other people.

Women can't gain equality until men get on board with gender equality. As a woman, I know we all struggle with sexism and I don't think any woman is too privileged to experience sexism.

I like things that are a little bit Victorian or 1920s, or cabaret, and are sort of magical and fantastical. I used to be a dancer and I took ballet really seriously. I was always in theatre and I love musicals. Old musicals have formed my style. I like anything that looks ballet-ish, Harlem renaissance-y, or of the jazz age.

I'm a fan of having a theme every day. So if I'm knee-deep in really political stuff, I have my revolutionary outfits.

The Citizens Band is a political theater group I founded. We try to create a fantastic Never Never Land that exists somewhere between 1880 and 1943. I look for songs from the early 1800s that speak to the political situation going on today. I'm big on the universal drama and that's sort of what The Citizens Band is based on. As humans we repeat the same mistakes over and over again and we certainly can't learn from them unless

The burden for caregiving really falls on women and until we address that, equality between women and men is not going to happen. In order for that to be rectified—instead of telling women to lean into their career or be more like men, or work harder—I think we need to tell men to lean into family life and domestic life. I think we focus so much on raising feminist girls and as a parent I find it frustrating that we don't focus as much on raising boys who can live outside the box of prescribed masculinity. What we expect from men is as oppressive as what we expect from women.

When I think about what the standard of beauty was even twenty years ago, and then I look around now, I realize beauty is anyone who's living their true essence, who's vibrating something that's true to them.

Activism and politics and changing paradigms also have to be fun.

I'm a fan of having a theme every day.

Andrew Logan

I'm interested in taking something that's in the gutter, like a rusty old bit of tin, and embellishing it. I can make something that's very humble look like a million dollars. I like to transform.

Lindsay Degen

I feel less obliged to do a collection every season because I find it to be more and more wasteful. This time 100 percent of my collection was recycled. I'd like to make fewer, but higher quality, items. I don't understand why companies that have so many resources wouldn't use them to do something good. I'd like to run a knitting facility and take in disenfranchised people and have them build it with me.

Your body is advertising what you're endorsing.

Taz
Arnold

107

Wamuhu Waweru

DESIGNER, CURATOR, ACTIVIST
LOS ANGELES

I want to make sure that what I buy is going to local people who can use it for their families and to elevate their communities.

I grew up in Nairobi, Kenya, so I'm a big-city girl. In Kenya, there's really no middle class, so we were upper-poor, which means we had something to eat every day. It was a beautiful place to grow up. We played outside, we sang and stayed out until dark. Until I got to know rich people, I never thought that we were poor.

Indigenous things are my passion and calling. I like to travel and find different pieces. I work mostly with women who are making crafts as they have in their tribes for generations. My way of supporting them is economic and helping them be sustainable is a way to celebrate the culture but also to preserve it. Globalization is watering down a lot of indigenous people's crafts and we're going to lose these things if my generation doesn't wear them. The textile industries in Kenya are pretty much dead because everyone is getting cheaper stuff from China.

I'm not into cultural appropriation, but I'm ALL for CULTURAL APPRECIATION. knowing what the pieces are and giving them the REVERENCE they deserve.

I don't want to fund oppression. If we make better choices about how we consume and refuse to buy manufactured products, then companies will have to change. Now they don't have any incentive to change because everybody is still buying their stuff.

I like being creative with my pieces. I definitely appreciate the ingenuity of the people who made them because they don't have much, and with the few things they have they always look like a million bucks, whether they're out farming, or tending to their cows—they're always wearing a beautiful piece. A lot of their jewelry has a meaning like, 'she's a married woman' or 'she's available.' But I wear them mostly aesthetically, I don't feel embarrassed to wear a marriage necklace. There's that whole question of appropriation. I think if appropriation becomes too sensitive and only certain people can wear a certain thing, then there's not enough demand for it and it dies.

Growing up I thought, 'Oh wow, I cannot be beautiful because all I see is very light-skinned, skinny white girls with long flowing hair.' But now, I feel so free and unapologetically beautiful and I can express myself in many different ways, whether my hair is short, long, in colored braids, or completely shaved.

If it makes you feel beautiful, that's a good enough reason for me. There's really nothing from my tribe that is traditional anymore, so I usually wear Maasai pieces. People could say I'm appropriating them. But they love it. Every time I go back home and show them pictures of the people who wear their crafts they're excited and really honored that other people enjoy them as much as they do.

With the bindi I wear, I get a lot of, 'Oh, cultural appropriation.' But, I do the bindi because I have a scar exactly on that spot. Usually the bindi goes on the forehead, but mine goes a little bit above my nose between my eyes. The lady who threads my eyebrows made me so comfortable with it. She's Nepalese, so she wears them for traditional and religious reasons and she told me, 'Oh, I love your bindi. You look so beautiful with it.'

The things made by hand with love are a drug because they also carry so much beautiful energy and wisdom. There's nothing new under the sun, I believe that we just transfer energy. It's a continuation, ashes to ashes, dust to dust—that same energy becomes something else.

Now I embrace every curve and kinky hair on my head. I've totally liberated myself from mental slavery.

Paul Manza

I'm amazed by craftsmanship, when things are created in honor of what they're being made for. There's a relationship, even if it's not conscious, between the designer, producer, and the wearer. These designers are touching my skin as much as any lover will touch my skin.

Ericka
Sance

I dont want to buy clothing that means nothing to me because that's like forgetting how to feel.

Adam Green

I wish people didn't treat everything like it was garbage. I wish clothes had cool little wind-y parts, and things that are handmade. I wish people kept their clothes for longer and fixed them. And I wish the whole world wasn't so disposable.

I'm comforted by the small. As long as I have a pen, paper, and guitar, I could live in a box for a year.

Heather Boo

Angel Clouthier

Why do people spend a month's rent on a bag, to make the people around them feel insecure? Women get a 'status bag' and stick it right on the table and show it off. It becomes the focal point, as opposed to who they are on the inside.

Molly Guy

There's something about being covered from head to toe that's sexier to me than showing a lot of skin.

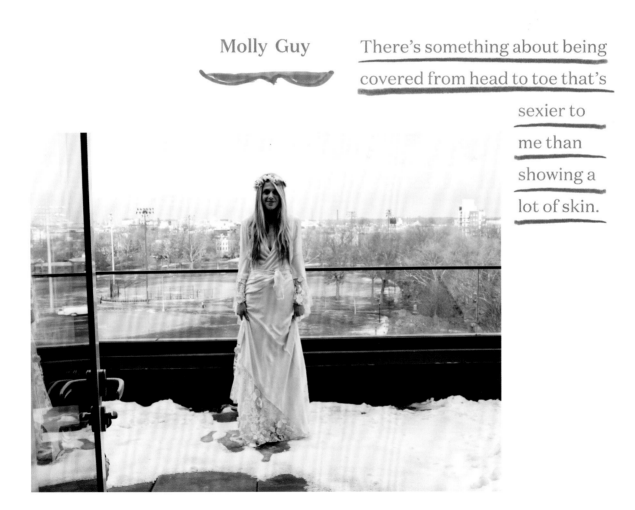

Leslie Crow

LEATHERWORKER, ARTIST, DESIGNER
AUSTIN

Our generation has an opportunity to go back to a more natural way of life, and that's something I am very passionate about.

I grew up poor in western Maryland and West Virginia in the Appalachian Mountains, with a lot of bikers and hippies and people that lived off the beaten path. My mom was an artist and my dad was a photographer. There was no sheep mentality. I come from a long line of really strong, independent people who do whatever the fuck they want.

I learned from my parents to broaden my horizons and to believe that nothing could hold me down. Just because we didn't have money, that didn't mean I couldn't do the things that I wanted to do because there's always a way.

Leaving Los Angeles was a really hard decision. My two best friends and I have our business, Heyoka Leather, based there. But I realized LA just wasn't inspiring me anymore. It was distracting me from creating art. The isolation that comes from living out here leads me to create nonstop.

Everything I make is from deer and elk. Someone hunts the animal for food for their families and instead of leaving the hide to deteriorate in the

field, they bring it to the tannery and we get the finished product to turn into our bags. There's no compromise. If it's not hunting season and we don't have enough materials to make the order, then we'll put people on a waiting list. Most people who make leather bags use deer-tanned cowhide to get the effect of deer skin. But then you are supporting the factory-farm industry and the giant

corporate food companies who can make a little extra money off selling the hides.

This jacket I just got recently here in Austin. It's from the 1940s. It's pony hair. The shirt was Angie's, my business partner. I think it was originally a dress, but then it ripped in half, so it became a skirt and a top. I got these boots at a swap meet. They were buried in this giant bin with hay and horse shit. I got them for $10. I wore them to go see Willie Nelson a couple of months ago.

I won't eat at McDonald's so I'm not going to use the cow hide that came from that slaughterhouse.

We grow all our own vegetables and eat only wild meat. I wake up in the morning around 7 a.m., collect eggs from the chicken coop, feed the donkeys, and clean up donkey shit. All of a sudden, it's eight o'clock at night and I haven't even eaten because I'm in the middle of ten projects at once. I'll be painting while I work on a leather bag and make jewelry on the porch.

Being able to have the average human stuff quiet down allows all my beautiful ideas that are lurking under the surface to come out.

If I like something, I'll hold onto it forever and wear it until it falls apart. I like things that have a story—something that can help you remember a person, an experience, or a memory.

Factory farming and the mass production of food—that's not the relationship we're supposed to have with our animal brothers. I didn't grow up living off the land. I grew up on macaroni and cheese in the box. Moving here, I have learned so much about growing my own food and living in a sustainable way that leaves a minimal impact on the world.

There's so much freedom in being alone. A lot of people are continually distracted by their phones, the TV, their friends, or whatever they surround themselves with. I think a lot of people are scared to look inside their souls and really get to know themselves.

I'm still wearing the clothes I've had since I was sixteen.

Nothing cures all the bullshit like sitting on a mountain for four days just praying and finding your inner strength. That's the salvation for everybody—if you can find your inner strength and be confident that your path is the right one, then you don't give a fuck what everyone else is doing.

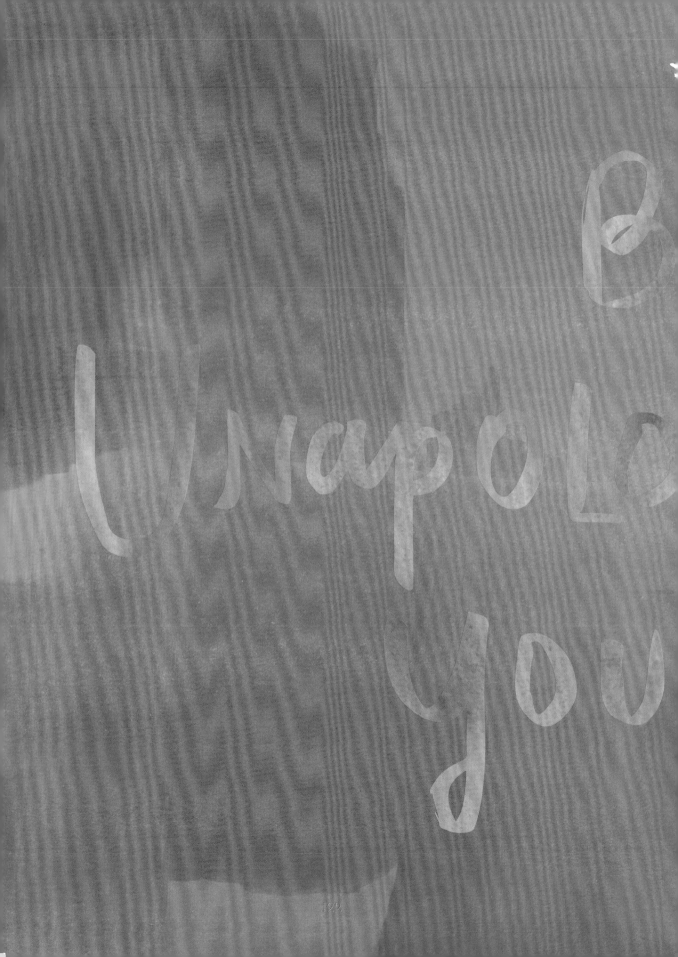

& Unapolo you

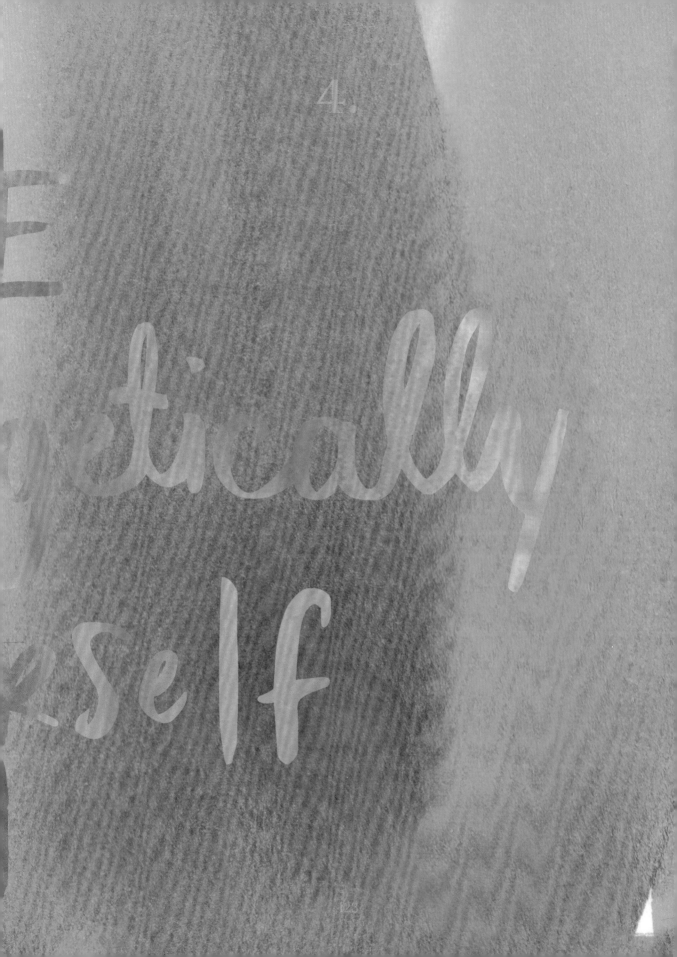

4.

...etically

...self

I, Elisa, am nearing 60 and if I lived by society's standards of what a 60-year-old woman 'should' do, wear, and behave like, my life would look completely different than it does right now. When I started StyleLikeU in my early 50s, it was a complete and utter reinvention. I left behind a lifetime of experience working in the traditional fashion industry for an ambiguous internet video start-up, something I knew next to nothing about. Most people thought I was crazy. The truth is, it was the best decision of my life and the reason I am writing this book.

In fact, defying stereotypes of how a person is 'supposed' to behave or look has become somewhat of a pet cause for me. I have always been rebellious by nature. I disdain arbitrary rules and I relish breaking them.

This doesn't mean that I don't suffer at the hands of the prescriptive messages that our culture thrusts upon us every day. When it comes to aging and my career, there have been times where I've been riddled with anxiety at being a beginner again in the second half of my life, taking a nontraditional path at a stage where many of my peers are settled and secure.

But what I've discovered through our interviews is that most of the things society and the media tell us we are — too old, too passionate, too artistic, too weird, too sexy, too modest, too gay, too straight, too feminine or not masculine enough—are made up prisons that we

don't have to lock ourselves in. What's more, the moment we stop subscribing to these expectations, they vanish altogether.

As an example, this chapter features Dynasty and Soull, who challenge gender roles. While these twins present as what's often considered 'Aggressive' or 'Femme Aggressive' within the lesbian community, they reject these labels and the limiting connotations that come with them. Instead, the maverick sisters are writing their own script of what it means to embody both masculine and feminine energies, allowing them to fluidly express their human wholeness.

Despite the outside messaging, deep down I feel so fortunate to have found my calling at this stage of my life, no matter the unorthodox route I took to get here. Each bump in my road has helped me learn how to fiercely follow my own voice.

So let your freak flag fly, and don't make any apologies about it. If you are going to follow any rules in life, make them about not comparing yourself to others, changing who you are to fit in, or trying to be someone that you're not. As renegade stylist B. Åkerlund says in this chapter, 'people need to realize that they have to be who they are. If you're trying to be someone else, it ain't gonna happen.'

B. Åkerlund

FASHION ACTIVIST, STYLIST
LOS ANGELES

People NEED to Realize That they have to Be WHo they ARE. If you're trying to be someone else, it ain't gonna happen.

I moved to LA in the 8th grade. All the girls wore Guess jeans and I totally didn't fit in. I was the shyest one out of all my friends and it was hard for me to talk in a crowd. I found my expression through my clothing. Clothing was my language; it was my way of being present without having to open my mouth.

When I was 18, I became a waitress, I dyed my hair blue, and I got fired. I feel like everything in life leads to something else, because if you don't like my blue hair then I guess I don't need to be here. I had a million wigs, and my friends and I used to dress up and go to lots of clubs. Every penny I got, I used to buy clothing. A photographer who shot drag queens lived next door to me and said, 'You should be a stylist.' I asked, 'What's that?' He said, 'It's what you already do, you just do it for other people.' He asked me to style the drag queens he was shooting for a calendar. I used everything in my closet, I had everything I needed.

The thing is, people say, 'You're so lucky.' Screw you... I'm not lucky. I worked for free. I lived off of ramen noodles and seaweed in an apartment with a roommate that was the size of my living room. I've been told my whole career that you have to be in New York if you want to be some-body. But you don't have to be any-where. You just have to be who you are.

At one time, my dream was to do the cover of *Rolling Stone*. Then the phone call came: 'Can you fly out to New York to do the cover of *Rolling Stone* with the Beastie Boys?' That was my goal, now I'm there, so I need a new goal.

Then Madonna asked me to style her half-time performance for the 2012 Super Bowl Halftime Show, which involved over 400 people. I spent three months working on the 11-minute show with her, and it was the biggest challenge of my entire life, because it was watched by 120 million people. Madonna came out as a modern-day Cleopatra. After it was done, I went into a cocoon for two months. I had given it my all and I was empty inside. But Madonna taught me that

when you think you are good, you can do better; when you think you are done, keep going.

My children had cribs covered in Swarovski crystals, because I was so deprived of being creative when I was pregnant and not working that I crystaled everything they had. They looked like pimps. After giving birth, the first job I had was on Lady Gaga's 'Paparazzi.' I literally exploded. I hadn't worked in a while and I had a lot to say.

Sometimes, when I pick up my kids from school, the other kids look at me like I'm crazy. People have asked me, 'Are you a witch? Are you a vampire?' I may not look like other moms, but, to Billie and Eddie, I'm just their mom.

I'm still wondering what I'm going to be when I grow up. I still feel like a kid. I'm proud, my life is just starting. I see myself growing old with my husband in the south of France, living in a chateau, running our own bed and breakfast, Åkerlund Hotel, with memories and memorabilia from all of the journeys and jobs I've had.

With everything soft, there needs to be something hard. I'm rock 'n' roll—I can't be too hippy-dippy.

When I travel, I have ten suitcases. It's ridiculous but I need options. Anything can happen, I have to be ready.

Michelle
Elie

You can't please everybody.
If you're for everybody, you're
for
nobody.

Jordan
Bradfield

I like the idea of
taking something that
someone would think
is feminine, adding a
masculine touch and
having an aggressive
undertone to my look.
It makes someone look
at me and say, 'I really
want to call you a faggot,
but then I'm afraid you
might kill me.'

Illona Royce Smithkin

I've come into my own quite late in life. I'm a late bloomer. You have no idea how insecure I was, I didn't think I could do anything right. I just didn't believe in myself.

Now I know who I am.

I've realized you don't have to change things about yourself, you just have to accept things.

Oh Land

I definitely had that time in my life when I tried to fit in more. When I look at those pictures I think: Ugh. Now it's as if I've gone back to what I was when I was kid. I've become more and more my 6-year-old self.

Betsey Johnson

I got sent home when I went to get married in my beautiful Victorian velvet pantsuit in '67 because they wouldn't marry me in pants. I came back in a crotchy miniskirt, the shortest little suit.

It's either my way or the highway. I like to play like that.

Devendra Banhart

ARTIST
LOS ANGELES

My alter ego as a woman freed me to sing. I felt like I had been given the keys.

For my birthday one year my mom gave me a Rolling Stones tape. I wanted to sing like Mick Jagger but, as a boy, singing didn't make sense to me. Then one day when nobody was home, I went into my mom's room and tried on one of her dresses. I combed my hair a different way, looked into the mirror and sang.

A lot of people are scared to dress the way they want to or in a way that makes them feel empowered and beautiful. When I see a trans person, it is one of the most beautiful sights to me. For some reason, black trans men hit me the hardest. It just takes so much balls to say: I am going to wear daisy dukes, lipstick, and be strong and proud of myself.

I remember, one day, just to see how I would be treated differently based on my exterior, I wore a suit to school. The reaction? Not much. Then I wore a torn shirt with smeared lipstick and my hair slicked to the side. The next day I wore baggy pants, Timberlands, and a Gap sweater. I also slicked my hair back and wore a pearl earring. Girls started noticing me, asking, 'Hey. What's up?' A guy in the hallway gave me a high five. These are people who had never ever talked to me before, which was interesting. The next day, I wore a basketball jersey and the reaction was totally amazing. People who had never ever recognized my existence were saying, 'Hey. How you doing?' On the last day, I wore a dress. It seems like a small deal (kids probably go to high school in drag now), but at the time, in high school it was a big deal for me and for the high school. Luckily, I made it through without being beat up. I also wore shirts that said HOMO. I got in trouble for that. It wasn't me trying to offend anyone. I was trying to make a statement about how we're judged so much by what we wear.

You need to feel comfortable in what you wear, but what makes you comfortable changes. So the most important thing is making peace with yourself. When making music, I am certainly at my most present. And that is a lot closer to making peace with myself than making war. It seems absurd to me to be at war with myself

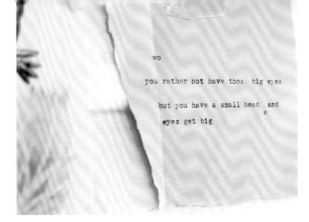

wo

you rather not have thos big eyes

but you have a small head and

eyes get big

when I'm in the present. The more I fail with each record, the more I want to put into the next one. If there is a great sense of failure, it's wonderful to me because that's an impetus to go in and make a new record. I don't necessarily like the music I make, but I love making music.

I don't have the good sense to avoid those things that I will regret, even in my sense of style. If you tell me that the fire is going to burn my hand, I am going to burn my hand anyway.

Dynasty and Soull Ogun

CONCEPTUAL DESIGNERS
BROOKLYN

Our parents let us explore. We were never forced to look a certain way to appease anybody.

— Soull

Soull

I express both masculine and feminine by being who I am. I don't really see a line between the two. If I'm attracted to a certain piece of clothing, that speaks for itself. I can wear a man's suit or shave my head, but I still have my period and I still have breasts. If you went into my closet, you wouldn't know whose closet it was because there's nothing in it that is 'woman' or 'man.'

At seventeen years old I gave myself the name Soull. My birth name starts with S and my last name with O, and then the U and L stood for Universal, Lesbian Lover. I was 'lesbian lover' because I was playing along the lines of, "Okay, I guess I'm an aggressive because I'm attracted to women who look like women and I'm not attracted to women who look like men.' So I thought I had to dress more masculine, but then after a while I realized, no, that doesn't really work for me.

The gay community that Dynasty and I were affiliated with was more like, 'Are you an AG?' Which is aggressive. 'Are you a Femme, are you a Fem-Aggressive?' But we didn't really fall within the lines of any of those. Ultimately, gay communities still try to resemble heterosexual lifestyles. They are still oppressed by the system. So, changing my name to Soull was conceited and pretentious, but ultimately it was me trying to free myself from the boxes of the gay community.

I remember when I was nineteen or so, my first girlfriend's mother said, 'You remind me of Grace Jones.' And I thought, 'Oh my god, I can't believe she said that.' At the time mainstream was all about soft-skinned whiteness and Grace was the epitome of masculine, un-dominate-able androgyny. So it didn't feel like a compliment, because it made me feel unattractive in my blackness.

Now I find strength in my masculinity and I see that beauty and ugly are one and the same.

Dynasty

I think feminine and masculine are energies in the middle that flow back and forth. I like the mystery, I'd like people to want to discover those aspects about me. I have a resistant energy to what's popular. If everybody's into one energy, I want to go the other route, because I'm pretty sure there's something out there that hasn't been touched yet.

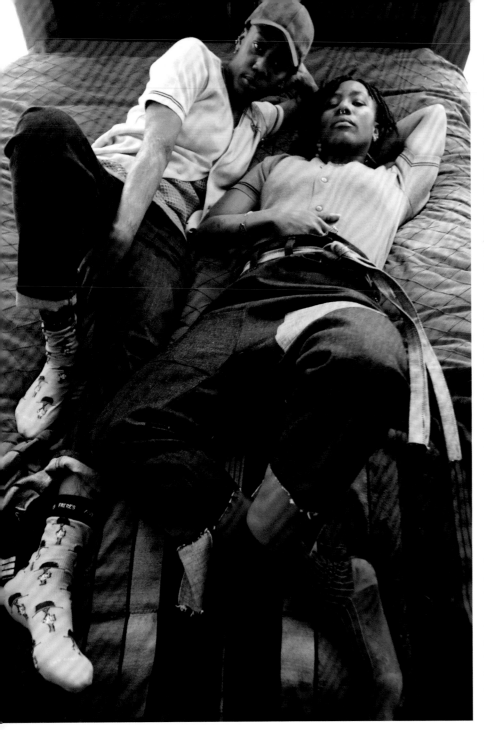

I really wanted to understand why I was the way I was. Soull was a little more feminine than me, and it was more accepted. And she dated guys. I was sneaking around talking to girls when I was sixteen, exploring these social media chat rooms. I was wearing triple-X jerseys, size 36 jeans. It was baggy, and not cute baggy. But I still didn't feel free because I felt like I was covering up a lot.

I grew up with people staring at me. I've always felt that I had to defend my image, so I started going by Dynasty. I took on this name that was genderless. It came from a place of anger, defensiveness, fear, and retaliation. As in, if anybody messes with me they're going to 'die nasty.' But even though it came from chaos, it was still beautiful because I used it to transcend myself. Now I've been Dynasty half my life and I've actually started to become Dynasty, more knowing of herself, more clear and focused on what her purpose is, which is to transform from coal into diamonds, or from caterpillar into butterfly.

Our bodies are vessels for expression. I came here as a female-bodied woman, but the way in which I use this vessel is up to me, because I am whole. So I'm masculine in expression, even if I'm a woman. When I started studying energy and roles, and what women are and what feminine energy is and how it's suppressed, I started to embrace it. I thought, "It must be powerful if everybody on the planet wants to suppress it."

I've always been very masculinely driven, but I've gotten more in touch with my feminine expression as I've gotten older. Aesthetically, I've used clothing as a shield. I always wore my brother's clothing. And in high school when I started having the freedom to buy clothes for myself, I went straight to the men's department. I didn't understand my sexuality at that time. The clothing I got was to hide my figure that was starting to shape.

Soull

We used watermelons on our clothing because so many people connect with it as a symbol. But it's also used as a racial stereotype, part of portraying black people as lazy or eating a sloppy fruit, all of these derogatory things about the black community. Because in American history, selling watermelon was the first trade that free slaves were able to work in to make their own money. I wanted to dissect that. And to put it in fashion.

Our bodies are vessels for expression. I'm a female-bodied woman, but the way I use this vessel is up to me.

Dynasty

When we did the watermelon designs on our clothes, it helped to transform me. One day I was at the Chinese supermarket and they were selling cut watermelon, and I felt very self-conscious. When I walked in, I was feeling so high and mighty thinking, 'Look! They sell watermelon because black people are here.' That is self-hatred. You don't even realize you're doing it. You don't realize how deep it is. Black people eat watermelon in secret because they don't want people to see them. And I thought, 'Damn, that is so fucking weird to me.' So using watermelon on our clothing is a way to show that these things I've hated are actually really dope. I am breaking the stereotype because I feel free when I wear it. I'm able to transform the watermelon to represent freedom.

Mariah Malakapua

I didn't ever consider the limitations others thought I should have because I was a young single mom. They said, 'Oh, you can't finish school.' 'Oh, you can't go traveling around the world backpacking.' 'You should become a dental hygienist.' I screamed, 'No way!' I have to be authentic to what my path is, and my path is leading a much more radical life.

Alec Friedman

People say to me upon meeting me, 'Oh you're Not gay?' or 'oh, you're Not French?'

As a Feminine Man in this World, you're somewhat powerless until you create and harness your POWER.

Armen Ra

145

I had no chance of being normal, so I always tried to own my weirdness.

Amy
Van
Doran

PROFESSIONAL MATCHMAKER
BROOKLYN

I grew up on a junkyard with my with grandma and grandpa, because my grandpa was an anarchist junkman. My grandparents collected all the weirdos. If they were building a fence, the one-legged man would come over and make the hole in the ground. They were King and Queen of the Misfits. I felt like a fairy growing up in the woods.

My grandma is from a circus town, Sarasota, Florida. Everyone in her high school was trained to be in the circus and she became a tightrope walker. Her friends included bearded women and giants. She was one of first ladies to wear pants. She was a badass with a motorcycle. She'd go into the yard and howl at the moon like a wild animal. My grandma was a nudist. She had giant pendulous breasts. My friends would come over and she would be in the kitchen cooking her witches' stew completely naked. My grandma used to dress me up like I was her Victorian doll. She would take the curtains down off the rods and wrap them around me, adding ribbons and giant hats.

She was so theatrical in her dress that I grew up thinking that a costume was the same thing as regular daytime clothing.

People shouldn't be homogenous. If you're a weirdo, then be the weirdest person that you can be.

I don't like one-size-fits-all generic mentalities and personalities.
I really like the broken weirdoes and the obsessive-compulsive types,
the people who are really good at one thing and bad at another.

Charlotte
Kemp Muhl

I don't like pants, because I actually find they're less tomboyish. I can move around faster in a dress.

Tat
Vateishvili

IF You feel comfortable
without looking in a mirror,
then you know you're not
embodying anybody else.

Justin
Tranter

We don't wear a costume, we
wear our lives. I would rather
people love
or hate
something.
The worst
thing I
could be is
average.

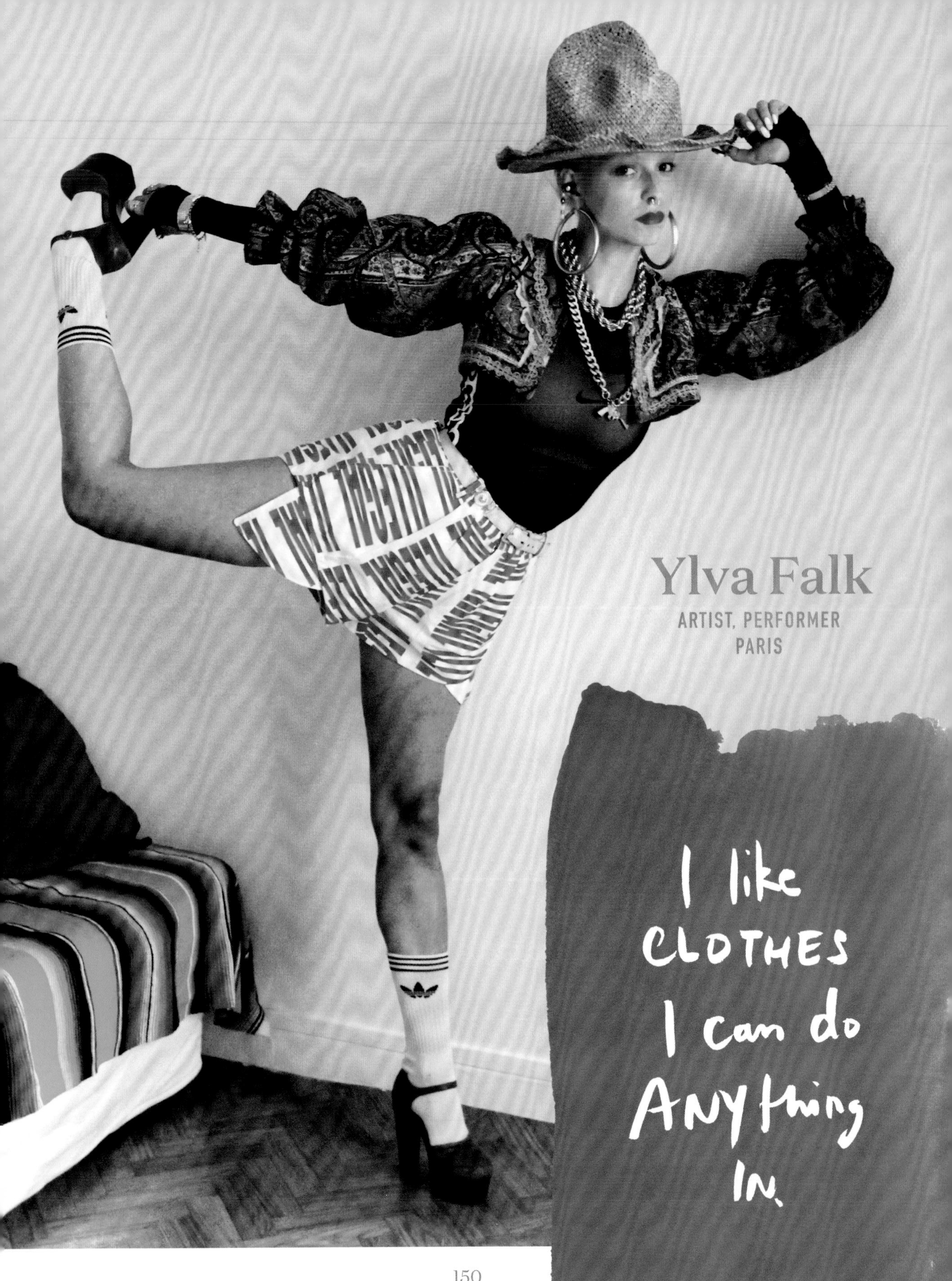

Ylva Falk

ARTIST, PERFORMER
PARIS

I like
CLOTHES
I can do
Anything
In.

I'm from a village in Sweden where there are three houses and the rest is forests. My parents were green-wave hippies, and I felt alone and different. When I was five, I found old-lady high heels in the vintage store. I always dreamt of being a diva.

At 16, I moved to Gothenburg, a bigger city in Sweden, for dance school. My life was dance. But I was a control freak and not eating. I wanted to fit in, to be good at dance, and to be loved. People couldn't see it, because I looked so free-spirited, but I wasn't.

My two loves in the dance world are ballet and breakdance, so I have always had a very strong feminine and masculine side, even in my style.

A lot of people in Sweden are perfect looking. They have perfect skin and bodies, and everybody looks so beautiful. It's weird . . . I didn't feel ugly, but I just felt so stiff in between all of these perfectly styled and relaxed people. I was having panic attacks and going to therapy. I felt like I had to leave Sweden, go somewhere where I didn't know anybody.

Paris needed me and I needed Paris. The people that are outsiders in Paris are different 100 percent. They are real freaks with real style.

This is my view of a princess, it's probably a '50s cabaret dress. The leg opening makes the dress ghetto in a way, but it's still sophisticated. I want people to think that they have seen it before, but, really, they haven't at all. I'll be naked, but my teeth will be painted black, so you think I'm super sexy and disgusting at the same time.

There is an oppression that makes men afraid to be beautiful.

Nelson Campbell

But it's okay for guys to be pretty. Style is one of the easiest ways for people on the street to look at you, and say, 'What?!' and question their whole system.

Carmen de Lavallade

You realize your body is changing and you have to accept, 'Okay, I'm 83.' At this age, it's an experience. In a way, as hard as it is, if you don't have these challenges, your brain isn't challenged, and therefore the body isn't challenged. So my whole thing is: How far can I go?

Ashley Smith

The fashion industry is based on judging people by how they look. I did not come from this world of fancy clothes or money. When I meet people who put me down or don't want to work with me because I am busty or have a huge gap in my teeth, it makes me laugh. I still have my life. I still have my friends and my sister. That is how I stay down-to-earth. Music and good friends is all you need.

153

Fatima Robinson

**CHOREOGRAPHER, DIRECTOR
LOS ANGELES**

My mom was into hardcore evangelism. I never wanted to go to church. When I went to clubs, I thought, this is where I feel the closest to God. So, if I feel this close to God, how can dancing be wrong?

I was always choreographing, but I never called myself a choreographer. I thought, 'How do you even spell that word?'

I didn't know there was an industry for people like me. People would see me dancing and ask me to do their music videos. It was the beginning of hip-hop. Back then, I didn't know that we were creating a whole world of fashion—a whole culture.

Out of the blue, I got a call from the director John Singleton. He had just graduated from film school and he saw me in a club and said, 'I'm going to put you in my movie.' So I got a call to be an extra in *Boyz N the Hood*. A couple of years later, John asked me to choreograph this music video for him that was going to be Egyptian themed. I asked him, 'Who's the artist?' He said, 'Michael Jackson.' I replied, 'Okay . . . perfect.' Then I hung up the phone and thought, 'Oh my God!' I was twenty-one at the time, and that sealed the deal for me to take it seriously.

I always felt like if I stopped doing what I loved to do in life then I wouldn't be a good mother.

I knew that choreographing was what I wanted to do. Street dance wasn't considered a true art form and I was passionate about making people respect hip-hop as a true art form.

I used to be on the train of: I have to do more and I have to be more successful. But that wasn't good for my soul. I was trying to rush instead of doing things in their proper time. When you do things in their proper time everything comes out flourishing. Go with the natural energy of your life.

I was so excited to get out of my 30s. The year I turned forty I went to Burning Man. Before I would have been too stuffy. Now, I feel like I'm at a place where I can allow myself to let go. This headpiece is from my Burning Man stash. I found it in a costume shop in Vegas. This was my Burning Man finale.

Magdalena Wosinska

PHOTOGRAPHER
LOS ANGELES

There's a thing that goes hand-in-hand with intensity and that's called passion.

People have always said to me, 'Oh my god Magda you're so intense.' I'm just like, 'Yeah but I wouldn't get all this shit done if I wasn't.' I used to get bummed about it and be defensive but now I think it's okay. Just because it's different doesn't mean it's bad. If I'm intense just accept me for who I am because I'll accept you for being lazy as fuck.

I started shooting self-portrait nudes when I was fourteen, because it was timeless and people couldn't judge me. They couldn't tell what music I listen to or social status I was in. When Instagram came out, I started posting that specific series on Instagram. It's so vulnerable when you're naked, and all I'm trying to do is express my lust for life and traveling and adventure and show that you don't have to be rich to travel. How much cooler is it to be naked under a waterfall or in a field of lilies than in a flannel and some shitty daisy dukes? I plan on doing this series forever through pregnancies, through everything as it starts sagging and falling apart.

I've NEVER WORN A purse in my life—my wallet, phone, and keys are somewhere in my socks.

I grew up really poor so fashion was never a thing for me, I always shopped at thrift stores. To this day even though I can afford a lot more, I'd rather spend my money on a good meal or a holiday. Half the time I don't even wear clothes, I'm naked. It's all about a good cowboy hat and boots.

I've always had a fear of not being heard because I didn't speak English when I first moved to America from Poland. I had to figure out how not to be shy and learn how to communicate. I was an outcast so I became a tomboy. I grew up skateboarding in the early nineties; girls did not skateboard then like they do now. Then I played in a metal band for eight years.

With photography, when I was assisting, guys wouldn't hire me because they thought I couldn't lift stuff, and I'd say, 'If it takes two dudes to lift something, it takes two girls to lift something.' And now, directing, it's still a bit of a boys club for sure. So I'm always putting myself in situations where I need to express myself, but I have to do it just as well as a man. It's something that's been ingrained in me.

Today I'm more feminine but I also race cars. I like pushing the boundaries. If I'm scared of the speed I think, well what can I do to overcome my fear?

I took the last three years to travel to soul search through those experiences because it was the first time in a very long time that I was not in a relationship. I had to face the fear—how do I travel alone? Traveling is very lonely

I'm afraid of heights, so I'll probably jump out of an airplane, even if I am terrified.

Today I'm more feminine but I also race cars. I like pushing boundaries.

and that time has been healthy because it's helped me to reflect and calm down. I'm no longer scared of doing certain things alone.

You're like, 'Fuck, I'm in the most beautiful place in the world and I have nobody to share it with and that's hard—and also that's great, I am here.'

I now feel that I have the ability to do anything I put my mind to, there's nothing that limits me. I've also softened up a little bit and and have stepped into my grace.

TURN
STRU
into SH

Your
ggles
rengths

In each interview that we conduct in our What's Underneath series, our subjects become more beautiful to us as they strip down, open up and disassemble the walls of their public personas. As the project has expanded, it's become abundantly clear that authentic style and beauty have absolutely nothing to do with projecting a facade of happiness or manicured 'perfection.' Rather, they rely almost entirely on an open heart, self-reflection, and the unshakable bravery to be yourself in a world that tells you that doing so is wrong.

One of the connective tissues in all of our interviews is that we simply can't shun, whitewash or conceal our struggles under a pile of faux positivity. We get that this may seem daunting, especially in a world that prizes happiness—or at least the image of it—above all else. But on the other side of fear is courage, and this message has been hammered home time and time again in our conversations.

Our subjects have welcomed every kind of challenge, confronted unthinkable adversity and hugged vulnerability at times when it's hard to imagine how they've done so. And the most beautiful part of it all is that it hasn't defeated them. Instead, staring down these hurdles has helped them each to find their distinctive grace. Confronting their personal battles has made them heroic, wise, and most importantly, unmistakably themselves.

In this chapter, we're putting the focus on some of these warriors who have valiantly turned their struggles into their strengths. Among them is supermom designer Gail Chovan, who embraced a double mastectomy (opting out of reconstruction) as an opportunity to prove that her femininity cannot be confined to any one physical trait. Also featured is Cipriana Quann, a leader in the natural hair movement who has taken the pain of domestic abuse and created an online platform for black women to support one another, reclaiming their self-expression in the face of Eurocentric beauty ideals. And finally, organic produce champion Renee Gunter has channeled abandonment as a child, five miscarriages and her experiences with systemic racism into the impetus for nourishing others by opening the first natural food market in her hometown of South Los Angeles.

We can't skip ahead to a happy ending or live inside a photoshopped image or an Instagram filter. There is no finding one's self when glossing over the truth. What's Underneath has taught us that our struggles form the foundation of our identities, and that real strength is found when you own your life and everything about it— the good, the bad, and the so-called ugly.

Gail
Chovan

DESIGNER, ACADEMIC
AUSTIN

I had beautiful, perfect breasts. When I learned they had to come off, I thought, 'So they come off.' I'm moving forward, this is who I am now.

I'm not the mom who drops my kids off in yoga pants or running shorts. I have nine-year-old twins who are quirky and magical. My son, Creed, wakes up in the morning and puts on a necklace and a Moroccan jalapa and goes to school. The other kids, wearing their athletic attire, tell him, 'It's not costume day.' I hope that spirit is never squashed by social constructs.

167

My daughter, Zelda, on the other hand, is blind, so it's fun to see how she relates to clothing. We have this expression in our house, 'Zelda hugs the homeless.' We'll go out on the street, she'll meet someone, and she'll pat them and hug them and say, 'Hi, how are you?' It's all tactile. Her style is spreading this magic.

She's a magical, magical child. And for somebody to think that Zelda's missing out on a huge part of life because she can't see . . . Sure, I look at a tree and I think, 'I wish Zelda could see that.' Or rather, 'I wish I could see the tree the way Zelda can see it.'

Both kids were born with congenital toxoplasmosis, which is a parasite that affects the eyes and the brain. They have shunts in their brains, which drain cerebrospinal fluid down their necks in tubes that go into their abdomens. Zelda also has a seizure disorder.

The biggest influence in my life has been my husband. I finally found somebody who understood me and wasn't afraid of me. We've been through so much, especially in the past nine years, between cancer, the kids being born early, both of my parents dying, and Zelda who had 11 brain surgeries. Our family turns it into a strength by showing that we're not beaten, that we're still going.

My decision not to have reconstruction after breast cancer was more about confidence as opposed to insecurity. Neither my mom nor my sisters had big breasts. Growing up, we all had different views on that. I saw it as this beautiful advantage of never having to buy a bra. My mother said, 'Wear a padded bra so you're more feminine.' I thought, 'I'm feminine, and I don't have to wear a padded bra to show that.'

My body is a roadmap of everything I've been through. Do I mourn my body? Yes. My ovaries are gone, my breasts are gone, but now it's a new chapter. I'm not a fucking survivor. I fought every minute during cancer. I didn't lie under a table and 'survive the bombing.' I was wearing great shoes and going to chemo.

I'm feminine, and I don't have to wear a padded bra to show that.

Our family turns it into a strength by showing that we're not beaten, that we're still going.

*I feel more secure with the insecure.
I've earned this for myself and no one
can take it away from me.*

$\dot{x} \rightarrow$

Elly
Mayday

This guy asked me, 'You're in New York by yourself? Aren't you scared?' And I said, 'I beat stage three cancer. What can I be scared of?' It's given me this warrior mentality. I proved to myself that beauty comes from within and confidence comes from within, it's something you give yourself. My body has brought me to hell and back.

I would choose this body again, even if it had cancer. Because it's mine.

Eryn Lefkowitz

I was prescribed ADD medication when I was nine. It got to the point where I wasn't eating because of it; I kind of knew I had an eating disorder but I was in denial. When my mom took action, I was 93 pounds. Since then I've gained 30 pounds.

Everyone was always telling me, 'You should model,' or, 'You have a sick body.' It was always positive reinforcement; no one ever said, 'You look so skinny . . . not so cute.'

Gaining weight has made me rediscover my body and what makes me comfortable. I thought I was going to be miserable, but I feel more graceful and serene.

Monica Canilao

ALL MY SCARS ARE PIECES OF ME AND I'M PROUD OF THEM.

They're like a visual journal of all the adventures I've ever had or the things that haven't killed me. They make me stronger.

Ryan O'Connell

I don't think anyone in this culture can be born gay and with cerebral palsy and love it, like, 'Yes! Gay and disabled?! Me?! Get out! Yeah!' No, you're going to be like Les Misérables because it fucking sucks, because you don't fit the mold.

When I started to not give a fuck anymore it was like this huge weight had been lifted off my shoulders. There were no secrets, no me going into a gay bar and hiding my limp. It was just like, 'Hey bitch, I limp, what's up, I have cerebral palsy. Google it, fuck off.' Shortly after that, I got a boyfriend. I was not receptive to love before, because I didn't love myself. The second I was like, 'Here I am,' boys came flocking. It was a real thing.

It's so fucking cool to take a body that is not accepted by society and is not seen as valuable and turn into the fucking coolest, strongest piece of work that I can.

Daphne Rubin-Vega

People would say, 'You don't look like an actor, you're never going to act,' because actors didn't look like me. My stepfather would say, 'You know, people are going to think you're stupid, just by the way you look. It's not an even playing field. Because of your race and your class, you are going to be judged. So you have to be smarter.' And I always remembered that.

Zoe Dolan

I always knew that I was in the wrong body because I always felt uncomfortable in my own skin. All of sudden, I realized that I really could transition, that it was worth getting surgery to be me. I took the New York bar exam, then scheduled my surgery in Thailand. My first thought when I woke up was, 'Why are all these Thai nurses around my bed giggling?' One of them pointed down and said, "beautiful," and I just thought, 'Oh wow, I get to be beautiful now. I get to give it a shot.' I finally feel comfortable enough in my body that I can allow myself to fall in love, to be vulnerable and to let go.

Cipriana
Quann

CO-FOUNDER, URBAN BUSH BABES
BROOKLYN

My Hair is the physical evidence of my Confidence.

I was modeling for years, and one of the things that would always come up was the kinky texture of my hair. There would be a conversation about straightening it or manipulating it into loose curls—whatever they deemed as being more commercial or more beautiful. I reached a point where I had enough. My mother is my idol and her hair is like mine. People telling me that my hair wasn't beautiful gave me this weird sense of: 'So you don't think that my mother's hair is beautiful?' It hit home.

I have an identical twin sister. We're best friends. Our dad was very strict, while on the other hand, our mother was very loving. In our household our mother was the breadwinner. She was the one who was working, going to school. Our dad was the homemaker and the one that was raising us. He was physically abusive. I don't mean occasionally physically abusive. We were dealing with it every week until we were about fourteen years old.

One day my dad got into one of his rages. He was threatening to harm my sister and wanted to know where the gun was. I'll never forget it, my mom walks in with my dad standing there with a gun in his hand. She asked him very calmly if he could go to the store to get her something. As soon as he left, we got in the car and went to an IHOP. When we came back to the house, my dad was gone. While we were at the diner my mom had him committed to the psychiatric ward. It all happened so quickly. My sister and I started to tell my mother what had been going on for all these years. I remember the look on her face. I could see all the guilt weighing on her, which is exactly what my sister and I didn't want to happen.

Seeing the true empowerment of my mother inspired Urban Bush Babes. When she saw that her children were in danger, she reacted quickly. This

affected how I feel about being protective and encouraging to women. I love to see women succeed. Our site is a platform for women to feel comfortable being themselves, a place where they aren't scared of what other people think or of what is going on at home.

I wasn't going to let my past decide who I was. I didn't want to be hateful or carry any anger.

I'll never forget it and I'll always appreciate it, but I didn't want to let it hold onto me. All those things that happened in the past have made me stronger, more aware, and more humble.

The real strength lies in how you overcome it. Even if you fail, get back up and do it again — that's life.

177

Bethann Hardison

• • • •

Too many people in the fashion industry are still sleeping at the wheel when it comes to diversity. Their arrogance is getting really annoying.

THIS isn't senior citizen time for me. The revolution ain't over.

Lauren Wasser

I was lost being that cool girl, or pretty girl. I was that girl you wanted but you couldn't get. I ran away from love, I ran away from anything that was substance. As soon as I woke up from my coma I was a completely different person. I immediately wanted to apologize to everybody that I had done wrong or been rude to, I wanted to make peace.

If I hadn't lost my leg, my heart wouldn't be full. Now I have a purpose and I can make an impact in a positive way.

Latasha Alcindor

>—(◊)—<

I didn't have a lot of white friends at Wesleyan, which is a primarily white college. A teacher there told me I wasn't going to graduate because I came from a really bad high school. She told me I would need to work 40 times as hard as anybody, because I wasn't supposed to be here, I was a quota. When she said that, it hurt, but it also made me want to go hard to prove her wrong. I graduated and I gave the class speech.

For the rest of my life I'm going to be proving people wrong.

180

Karyn
Starr

My body is my vessel and it feels lucky as it's how I can experience love in this world.

I gave birth to a tiny baby that wasn't alive. I picked him up and he was so little and perfect. It was one of those moments where I thought, 'Wow, this is why people go so crazy.' But I eventually realized it just wasn't his time. Which was really helpful for me because I'm a spiritual person. I didn't want a scientific answer. And now I'm cooking this guy.

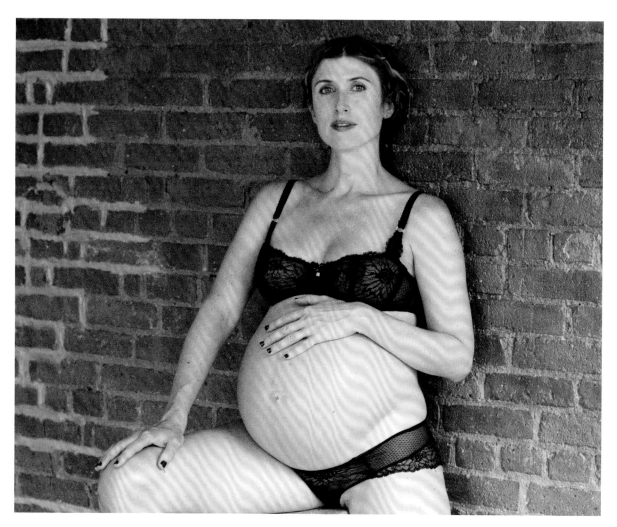

181

Cathy Cooper

ARTIST, MAKER OF STUFF
LOS ANGELES

What you wear says so much about self-worth. It's individualism on display.

I make very distinct choices in my style, and they're not safe. We live in a world where choices are made for us. It's really easy for people to get lazy about individual choice. Big corporate society, big mega stores—same clothes, same appliances, same everything.

I shot heroin for years because I wasn't willing to be present. A big part of addiction is blaming your pain on somebody else. Now I've been sober for twenty years. I'm a firm believer that I'm an addict, that I'm hardwired for it.

I was shooting so many drugs that my heart and my circulation were going. It was either stop or die. Nobody makes that choice but you. I got clean at my parents' house in the room I grew up in. Instead of copping dope morning, noon, and night, I wrote in the morning, exercised midday, and practiced with my band in the evening. If you want to make a big change you have to take big actions.

I feel the most
beautiful when I can
see the truth—
the essence of
what I am—in the art
that I've made.

My sobriety has driven the rest of my
life. Once you decide, that willpower
comes. It's not the other way around.
There's no power without decisions.

I feel the most beautiful when I can see
the truth—the essence of what I am—
in the art that I've made. What makes
it even better is if somebody else sees
that. That connection makes me feel
high—it's life-affirming.

Kelsey Lu McJunkins

Growing up as a Jehovah's Witness, whatever I wore was under a magnifying glass; nothing could be immodest. I was going to meetings and to church four times a week. My only time outside of that was for violin or cello lessons. My parents were extremely loving, but the idea of losing me to the world changed them. When my mom found out I was going away to music school, she beat me with a shoe; I had to bust out of my window and run. In this new world, music became everything. It was my way of expressing myself. Don't be afraid to be yourself. There's a reason for everything. How you're feeling about life shouldn't be ignored.

Jesse Kahweiler

Recovering from an eating disorder has taught me what it means to be a woman.

It's taught me how to take up space, inhabit myself in my body, confront my own shame, and deal with anger, control, and letting go.

187

Rachel Fleit

FILMMAKER, CREATIVE DIRECTOR
BROOKLYN

I get a lot of feedback about this baldness. When I'm walking down the street in New York City, people sometimes say, 'Nice haircut.' But I've never had a haircut in my life. I've had alopecia since I was 18 months old.

I wouldn't be who I am if I had long blonde hair. The depth wouldn't be there.

I used to be so ashamed of my alopecia. I didn't want anyone to know about it. It was a secret that I created. For fourteen years I wore a wig. I had bangs and wore really thick eyeliner so that no one would know I didn't have eyelashes or eyebrows.

People assume that I have cancer. In my 20s, I'd be smoking a cigarette and drinking whiskey at a bar and people would come up to me and say, 'I'm praying for you.' I'd say, 'Great! I need all the prayers I can get.' A lot of people think that I shaved my head. I always struggle with that. I'm not the kind of person who would shave her head. I'm a Jewish girl from Long Island. If I had hair, it would be long and lustrous. I wouldn't shave it off.

When I was younger, there was a lot of looking in the mirror and thinking, 'If I had hair, everything would be better. If I had hair, I would have a boyfriend.'

I stopped wearing a wig when I was eighteen. It was the most liberating thing. I had these great friends in high school, and the boys screamed, 'I'm gay!' and I screamed, 'I'm bald!' For the first time, I was able to talk about it. I took my wig off and my friends said, 'You look amazing, don't ever wear that again.'

<u>Letting go of that and being free and out in the world with no hair allowed me to settle into being me.</u>

Rafael Ramirez

Being black connects me to my culture, to a group of people who have experienced struggle and I think that struggle is such a beautiful thing because it pushes you, it challenges you, it makes you grow. Black is beautiful because of that resilience. Given my experiences and the things I want to do, I'm going to need that sort of resilience and strength.

Myla Dalbesio

I had a pill addiction that stemmed from body issues from working as a model. The agencies all said, 'We love you, you need to lose 15 pounds.' So I tried to lose weight. I was a size 6, the healthiest I've ever been. At one point, some guy gave me an Adderall for the first time. When I realized it made me lose my appetite, it became so hard to stop. Until one day when I hit bottom. I remember the moment, in my kitchen in Brooklyn. I was living with my boyfriend and trying to hide this addiction from him while trying to figure out how I could make the pills I had left last until I got my next prescription. Looking back, all my crisis moments have been the most important times in my life.

If you never had to struggle
or fight for anything in your life,
how could you know who you are and
what you're made of?

Jillian Mercado

I embraced my scars and mishaps in life and turned them into something awesome.

If you're different, that's sunlight in somebody's world.

Renée Gunter

MULTI-MEDIA ARTIST, DESIGNER
LOS ANGELES

I don't remember ever being told that I was loved. I had to love myself.

I was born and raised in Los Angeles to a mother who was 16 years old. I was abandoned, left alone in the house a lot, a vulnerable little two- or three-year-old, sexually assaulted by some of the people who came through. Who survives that kind of stuff?

As I grew up, I wanted to have a family and create that security and emotional continuity that I didn't have. I wanted to be a mom. I got pregnant when I was 18 because somebody said he loved me. Then, he wrote me off. I went to the doctor and the baby I was carrying had no heartbeat. That was the first of five children that I lost.

people crossing the street and clutching their bags, or not being served in a restaurant. Once I went into this well-known big-box store dressed in a tee shirt, jeans, and tennis shoes. The checker didn't even look at me. She just checked the merchandise. I wrote a check, and then she called the manager over. He okay'd the check and I left. Two weeks later, I came back. This time, my hair was up and I had some makeup on, I was wearing a little string of pearls, horseback riding pants, and some very nice boots. The checker asked me how my day was and if I

I became depressed and wouldn't get out of bed. One day, I woke up gasping, thinking, 'I've got to do something, because I am going to die.'

I adopted my daughter from a very courageous 18-year-old single parent who said, 'I am so glad to give you a girl because you deserve a daughter.' I've been jealous of my daughter at times because I never had the opportunity to experience the unconditional love that my daughter has had from me.

We lived in the San Fernando Valley, but I didn't see enough diversity there. People often thought that I was my children's nanny or a housekeeper. I got tired of

found everything alright. Two weeks earlier, it was assumed that I was a person trying to scam the system based on how I was dressed. Two weeks later, dressed in a thousand dollars worth of clothes, an assumption was made that I was of means and therefore not a threat.

Assumptions are made about me all the time, not just based on what I'm wearing, but more specifically on the color of my skin.

So I went back to the South LA neighborhood that I grew up in. People seemed a lot warmer and there was diversity. But within the first couple of weeks, a kid was killed on our street. I thought, 'Oh my God, where is my daughter going to go to school?' My daughter asked me, 'What are you going to do about it mom?' I said, 'I'm going to have a party.' I used the tools of the system and I blocked off the streets and had an old-fashioned block party. This was ten years ago. Only five people came initially. But last year, more than 700 people participated in it. I also thought a lot about food and security. I wanted to create a sense of community from the inside out. So I opened an organic produce market.

It's important to know who your neighbors are and to be the village.

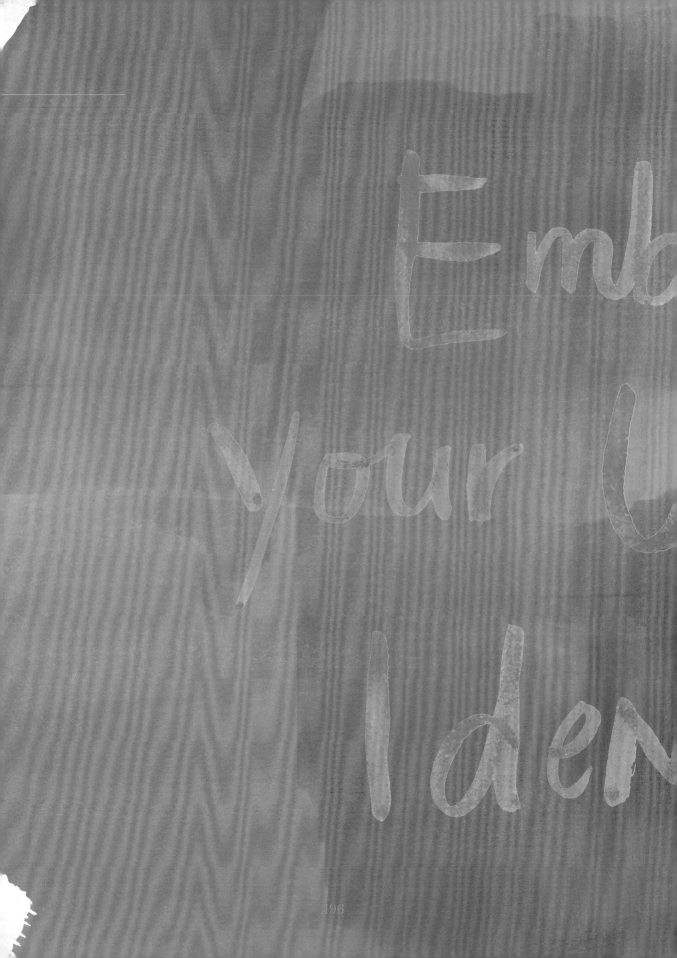

Emb
Your
Iden

RACE
NIQUE
TITY

6.

During our very first shoot back in 2009, our subject freed me. Before meeting Erica Yarbrough, I, Elisa, had always been a little embarrassed about my flat chest. I'd bought into the idea that small breasts equaled less sexy and therefore, with my size AA cup, my sexuality was somehow lacking. In her interview, Erica casually mentioned how much she cherished having no cleavage and how it perfectly accented her tomboy style. Suddenly, after decades of delusion, I was awakened to the idea that a flat-chested woman could feel as sexy as any *Sports Illustrated* swimsuit model. I went home, threw out all of my padded bras and, like Erica, made men's button-down shirts, open to the navel and sans bra, my go-to uniform. Suddenly, I felt sexier at 58 than I ever did as a self-conscious 20-something.

Ever since that day, it's been a fasten-your-seatbelt magic carpet ride as Lily and I have had our minds—and our staid ways of thinking about our bodies—blown with every interview. Each new subject that we've encountered—of all ages, sexualities, races, physical conditions, genders, shapes, and sizes—has pried our eyes open to the ridiculousness of our culture's sterile, binary ideal of what it means to be an acceptable woman, man, or person.

We've lost track of the number of times an interview has helped us understand that embracing, not resisting, something we've previously perceived as a flaw immediately transforms it into a treasured asset. Model Naomi Shimada, for example, turned growing out of her pre-pubescent, slender physique, something the industry punished her for, into her crowning charm. She leads with her curves and cites her mouth, the vessel through which she feeds herself, as her favorite body part. In a modeling industry laden with eating disorders, how bad-ass is that? By using her curvy figure to reinvent her career on her own terms, Naomi recognizes that what makes her different is not an imperfection, but rather a signifier that makes her rare and thus powerful.

So the mainstream ideal of beauty may change over time. It might be stick thin and blonde one day and small waist and big butt the next. But as long as we continue to believe there is any one ideal of what physical attractiveness means, we remain unable to express pride in the pure singularity we each possess. Feeling inadequate is a choice. As transgender activist Alok Vaid-Menon says in this chapter, 'I wasn't born in the wrong body. I was born in the wrong world.'

Alok
Vaid-Menon

ARTIST
BROOKLYN

The way I understand my gender is that I am both a man and a woman, and neither a man NOR a Woman. I'm outside these Categories.

I grew up in a small town in Texas. It was predominantly white, evangelical, Republican, straight, cisgender. I grew up with a sort of post-9/11 queer body, being told I was a terrorist every single day, being called a faggot every single day, being called a tranny.

I think so many of us who grow up in small towns think that moving to New York means we'll finally be acknowledged and safe, but that's a total lie. I've had people spit on me. I've had people call me an 'it.' I was getting off the train and this white man screamed, 'OSAMA!!!!' Then he looked down and saw that I was wearing stiletto heels. There was this really weird moment where I no longer fit his stereotype of a 'man-of-color terrorist.'

Women on the street harass me the most. I think it's because when women see me they're trying to protect this category that they belong to. When we talk about patriarchy, we talk about men doing it. But actually women also enforce patriarchy every day.

My fashion is its own form of armor; style is extremely political. My politics is, 'I am me. I am Alok. And Alok exists outside of your colonial white supremacist heteronormative gender binary.'

The core of misogyny against trans people, or transmisogyny, is that we're masquerading as something we're not—that we just put on this dress to trick someone. We are seen as worthy of the violence we receive. That's why people don't stand up for us. There's this idea: 'You chose to be that way, so you have to take the brunt of it.'

I see my hair as part of my femininity. If I have a beard and lipstick, that's part of who I am. Why do we always put the onus on people to change their bodies, and to prove or authenticate themselves to other people, instead of asking society to shift their norms?

The world I'm fighting for is one where we allow people to self-narrate their bodies— that's a profoundly radical act. We exist in a society that's invested in categorizing and creating norms about every single thing about us, rather than recognizing that none of us fit into norms.

I think one of my critiques of the trans movement is that it's been way more invested in language than in actual practical steps. I would like you to know my pronouns, but I'm much more interested in: 'Are you going to show up for me?'

I started writing poetry after my suicide attempt. Art is the space we go to when language fails us. How can we love each other hard enough so we don't have to outsource our trauma? We keep on making this mistake in the West where we think if we have more things we'll be happier, rather than recognizing that we already have everything we need. The way to move away from scarcity towards abundance is to recognize that we are enough.

I don't have to be
a woman or a man
to be coherent,
and that threatens
so much of the
fabric of this society.
I wasn't born in
the wrong body—
I was born in the
wrong world.

Meredith Graves

I was always the character actress. I was never the ingénue. I've grown up my whole life playing second fiddle to the pretty girl, and it took a really long time for me to realize that it's okay to be who I am — that in somebody's eyes, I might be the pretty girl.

Lysa Cooper

Black is beautiful because it's the one who is cast out. And isn't that one always the true diamond?

The true power belongs to the one less loved.

Lina
Esco

I wanted to understand why there isn't a female voice in the Bible. Starting Free The Nipple was what I had to do in order to initiate the dialogue of equality. Women are only topless at stripclubs or in porn magazines. Why aren't there healthy images of women owning their bodies—owning being topless? I wanted to do something radical, disruptive, that would change the way we think.

Reign Apiim

People walk up to me and ask, 'What religion are you? What country did you come from? Is this for something? Where are you going? Are you going to a ball? Are you a dancer?' I'm none of those things, I'm just living, it's just Wednesday.

If you're true to yourself, your life is already a fairy tale.

Grace Dunham

Before I used to understand trans to mean a very clear binary journey. You are one thing, it's not for you, you're trapped in the wrong body, and you go to the other thing. There are two options, and to be trans means to journey from one to the other. I am definitely trans, but I have learned that trans can be this expansive, unwieldy way of being. I'm accepting that I don't have a name for myself and that uncertainty is a more accurate and freeing reflection of who I want to be.

My favorite parts of my body are my mouth and my lips. All the things I love about life, like eating and kissing, come from them.

Naomi Shimada

MODEL, ACTIVIST, FILMMAKER
LONDON

I'm a plus-size model now, but when I was a straight-size model, I was always on the verge of being bigger. I always had boobs and hips, which ended up being part of the 'problem.'

When I was eleven, my family moved from Tokyo to the south of Spain, where I got scouted at a restaurant. I got signed to a modeling agency when I was thirteen. I was super tall and gangly, with long legs, long limbs, and long arms. I worked steadily until I was seventeen or so. When I finished school, I went to London to model. I went into the agency one day and they weighed and measured me and told me to lose weight even though I was already small. I was a US size 8. I shouldn't have been losing any weight. I've always been quite headstrong in certain situations, so I stopped modeling for a few years. Then I came back, and I got a few campaigns that wanted a busty girl.

But my body was changing and I just couldn't keep my weight down anymore. I tried everything to lose it. I tried exercise, hypnotherapy, every trainer, and every diet. It was so unlike me. I was suppressing my soul as a human being. I'd catch myself doing things that I never wanted to do. I'd see a friend and all we'd talk about is what we were eating and how we were losing weight. I didn't want to be that girl. I felt super dark.

Whenever I have anything that's too small for me, I give it away instantly. I want to live in the moment and not think: Maybe I'll fit into this one day.

And it didn't work. Now I feel like I look exactly how I'm supposed to look. As I get bigger, I carry the weight in a way that looks totally right for me. I come from this society in Japan where size is so frowned upon. If you're anything but tiny, you're a shame to the family. But my mom told us, 'I'll never be like that with you guys.' She gave me the attitude that there are other problems in the world that we need to focus on. There are bigger things than us. If we can change how we feel about ourselves in our heart and in our mind, then everything else will fall into place.

I'm actually at the heaviest I've been—a US 14 now. But none of the clothing that I wear is limited by my size. My roommate told me, 'You dress your energy.' I hope my energy is warm and full of love and vibrant. However strong I dress, my face softens it, I laugh all the time, and I'm very touchy-feely.

Juliana Huxtable

I used to hate my body. There were so many times when I didn't understand it at all. I felt like it was actively working against me. I felt exposed. But now I'm really happy where I am.

My body has given me a way of understanding how most people's idea of nature or normality is completely skewed.

Shaun
Ross

I'm black,
I have
albinism,
I'm gay,
I'm open,
these are
things
that I am. It's a lot, but
I don't lose myself ever.

DJ Louie XIV

My struggles with being in the closet, and my post-closet shame, initially held me back from my dreams, but now are fueling my work. I still have a lingering fear of my feminine side and, in my writing and acting, I'm dedicated to exposing that we have a society of gay (and straight) men who are terrified by their femininity. There is a dearth of real and nuanced gay guys in the media and that's a huge problem too. I think as gay men and artists, it's our job to put honest, not-clichéd images out there of ourselves and to thus stop being complicit in our own oppression.

Paloma Elsesser

'I don't see color'—that's wrong, you should see color. We are not the same. We have very different experiences.

You can fly your liberal equal flag, but shit is not equal.

Sarah Jane Adams

ANTIQUE JEWELRY DEALER AND ENTREPRENEUR
SYDNEY

I welcome the Aging Process.
I am an alien in this world,
I don't understand the rules.

My style is how I feel when I wake up in the morning. It's the clothes in my closet that I've gathered over the years. It's just my stuff — it's not my style, it's me.

The other night, an absolute sweetheart invited me to go to a gallery preview. But I don't have cocktail dresses, or any black frocks, or anything black in my wardrobe. My friend said that I couldn't wear sneakers or moccasins, but that's all I've got. I don't have sensible shoes and I'm not prepared to compromise.

I think when people look at me they assume I'm a complete ditz and totally chaotic. They don't understand why I don't shave my legs or have a manicure. So I look at people, and they're so surprised that this old woman is fucking looking at them. I'll smile; they don't necessarily smile, but they'll say, 'Nice kicks.'

Menopause started in my late 40s and it was very liberating. It wasn't something I wanted to hide behind or be ashamed of. What is the benefit in skipping over things? Then you don't learn the lesson.

220

I truly believe that the universe throws at you what you can cope with and the process of learning how to cope with it is how you grow. If you hide from what the universe throws at you, it will just throw it at you again in a different form.

Menopause can be something someone uses to insult you, like, 'Oh, you must be going through menopause.' But fuck off. That's what's good about menopause, you can actually say 'fuck off,' because before maybe you were too polite. Now I make decisions that are driven by a different set of hormones. I don't need to prove myself to anybody anymore.

What I love most about my body is my ledge. My ledge is there because I had twins and so for about two years I constantly had a child on this hip and this ledge developed. I love it because this is where my babies were.

My knees are getting saggy and my bunions are getting bunion-y but that's cool. It's my body, and it's more about the visualization of what's going on inside, which is that I'm getting older and happier and a bit more accepting.

The idea of what beautiful hair is is completely warped.

Lizzo

In Houston, where I'm from, people would say, 'Oh, I'm mixed. I got silky hair. I got good hair.' But good hair doesn't exist. I've spent so much money on weaves and braids, I could've bought two houses.

Jo Lampert

For me, the term 'androgynous' is good because it defies the boxes of masculine and feminine. I felt left out of the realm of what it means to be a woman, but now I embrace whatever my body is, which isn't this idyllic version of what a woman is. Now I'm realizing that can be exploded open.

My style says I have the AUDACITY to exist while everything out there is telling me I shouldn't.

Nikkiesha McLeod

224

I don't know
who I am, and
I'm okay with
that
uncertainty.

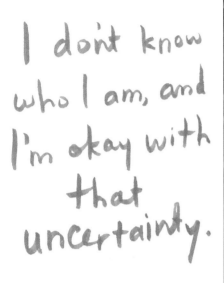

India
Menuez

225

Evan Voyles

I firmly believe that I am a better person at 56 than I was at 46. I may not be as physically capable, but I would never trade that for being more wise, experienced, and calm than I was at age 46, 36, 26, or 16.

Chloe Nørgaard

My agency told me that I should tone it down and be blonde, so I dyed my hair blue instead. I didn't want to just be a mannequin or a blank canvas in a black tee shirt and jeans at castings, I wanted to shine through. Then I found photographers, made my own book and kept pushing. It finally worked. I believed in myself and I knew it was possible.

Tyler
Ford

People see me as a boy they want to put in his place because boys aren't supposed to wear makeup, crop tops and miniskirts. As we grow up, we are groomed to fit into a certain box. Female turns into girl turns into woman, but it all starts with your body being labeled as female. That's not where we should start, we should start with a blank slate and grow up to be people and human beings.

For me being agender means not being confined by expectations or labels.

Ellen
Elias

People always say, 'Ellen, why do you dress like this? You will never find a man who's going to want to walk with you or talk with you.' But I feel like I don't have to look like girls in the magazines to have a man, and when I meet a man who sees this and accepts this, that's when I'll know I've met the one.

Ryley Pogensky

I didn't have trans role models to look up to, so I thought the closest I could get to being masculine was to become a 'butch' lesbian. The term 'lesbian' never fit me, though. I like women and I was born with a female body, yet I saw myself as man. But I didn't think I could be the trans kid. I was already gay, black, and adopted by white Jewish parents. I was the token of every token.

I had to sit down and push myself to deal. When I started transitioning, I became more comfortable in my body and could wear the clothes that I had dreamt of. Putting on a tie and blazer is like a badge of glory to me. Having someone on the street 'he' me means the world.

Sara Elise Hardman

I'll be in a group of mostly black women and I'm too white, and when I'm with mostly white people, I don't fit in because I'm of color.

I'm the way I am because I have multiple races, so there no need to silence myself to fit in with someone who doesn't have all of these gifts.

Stacy Barthe

Losing weight is the easy thing, it's the mental weight that's hard. I'm finally at a place where I can accept that I'm a work-in-progress, and I'm okay with loving me in the meantime. I'm forever becoming.

It's like being an unfinished butterfly, you'll never be complete, because completion is death.

iO
Tillett Wright
ARTIST, ACTIVIST, AUTHOR
LOS ANGELES

When I was six, I decided that I wanted to be a boy. A bunch of boys were playing soccer in the park and I wanted to play. They asked me if I was a boy or a girl. I told them I was a girl and they said I couldn't play. I was like, 'Fuck that, I'm a boy. Can I play now?' I then told my dad that, from now on, I wanted to be a boy. Everyone in my family said, 'We don't see you as a girl or a boy. We just see you as iO.'

I was born on 3rd Street and Bowery. My parents were all up in the No Wave Movement and drag culture. Everybody around them was inventing their identities so the idea that their kid would invent her identity wasn't strange to them. I had library cards under boys' names. It was a full immersive experience.

I was having this conversation with my project manager. He's 6'3", broad, hairy, and always wears nail polish. I asked him, 'What if I'm a man?' He told me, 'Look . . . I may wear nail polish, I wear makeup sometimes, and I'll occasionally be known to put on a dress, but when I go to sleep at night, I'm a man and I love being a man. I'm in my body and I love that.' I had a gender revelation, it's down to how you see yourself. I said, 'Then I'm a man.'

If I could just snap my fingers and tomorrow have a man's body, I would do it. I know what my body is and I'm clear on my genitalia, but I'm also fairly clear that, if transgender is how you feel on the inside, then I'm transgender. I feel like a man on the inside,

yet because of the way I was raised and never forced into dresses and all of that stuff, I don't have the narrative that apparently goes with being transgender, where you hate your body. I don't hate my body at all. And if hormones are going to change my mental chemistry and emotions, then I don't want to change that. So I don't fit into that box.

I've always thought of transgenderism as a physical in-between place and now I'm learning to understand it's also an emotional in-between place. What is a man? What is a woman? Much of that is society's bullshit, so why do I have to change my body to fit another norm?

I've had a rough and tumble relationship with my body and I love that. I love what my body is capable of. I love that there's nothing a boy can do that I can't do.

I NEVER Fit any box. I'm like the ultimate UNICORN.

CREAT

own D

of B

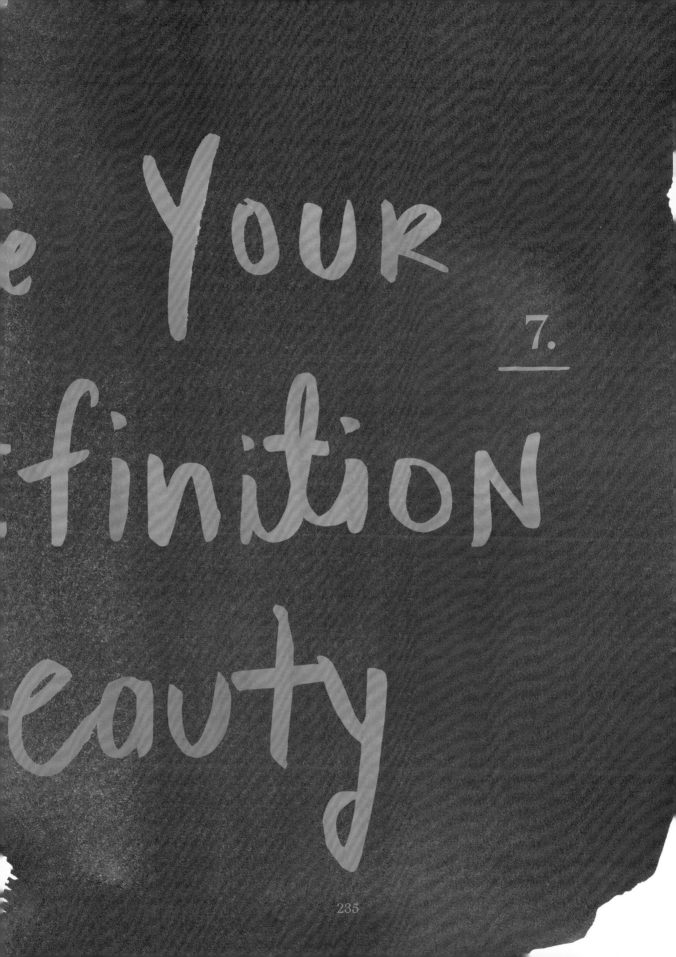

Your

7.

finition

eauty

235

My cousin told me recently, 'Lily, you look beautiful. You look like you've lost weight!' I smiled and responded, with love, that I don't take that as a compliment as I no longer equate being thin with being beautiful. I told him that I haven't, in fact, lost a pound in years—actually, I've gained a few. Any beauty he senses, I explained, is me radiating how comfortable I'm becoming in my skin.

Looking back, it is hard to remember the me of ten years ago, a girl who was completely consumed with trying to 'fix' the body she was born with.

Enchanted by the people I was encountering through StyleLikeU, I began to awaken from this trance. For the first time, I was exposed to robust souls who marched to the beat of their own drum in their style, their bodies, and in their lives. Awed by the vibrancy of their unapologetic spirits, I was determined to unlock that same sense of freedom in myself.

I began by rejecting any clothing that felt demoralizing. I threw away everything that fit me only during my 'skinny' days, and as a result, I stopped dieting and started exercising to feel good, not to alter my appearance. I began staring at my undressed body in the mirror and had my mom photograph me without hiding under loose clothes. Before starting What's Underneath, I'd almost never seen a positive representation of a body like mine presented back to me, so at first, looking at myself in this honest way was terrifying. But with time, this unfamiliar image became normalized. The same rolls, stretch marks, and cellulite that used to be the source of extreme angst, started to feel like home. It was a reprogramming of my mind and I was able to start to see my being through uncontaminated eyes.

Today, there is not a bone in my 200 pound, Amazonian body that I would trade with the waif I once wished I could be. This is not to say that I don't have my bad days—there are moments when I'm trying on swimsuits in a dressing room and old voices pop into my head, telling me there is something wrong with me. But when these occasions arise, I have the perspective to recognize that this is just a repetitive story. It is not the truth of who I am.

Perhaps no one exemplifies the ability to define beauty for herself as much as model Melanie Gaydos. She is the final hero in this book and is one of the most beautiful people we've ever met. Melanie was born with ectodermal dysplasia, a genetic condition that affects her pores, teeth and hair, among other things. Since she felt so far removed from conventional beauty standards, she was able to unearth a truth that actually exists for all of us—that 'beauty is no more than a feeling and state of being.'

My primary takeaway from my own metamorphosis and from those highlighted in this book is that we are never fixed. We each have the power to change our minds, and thus to create our own realities. Beauty is much more vast than we have been made to believe—and it can be accessed not by trying to change yourself to fit a mold, but by creating a new mold entirely.

Lisl Steiner

PHOTO JOURNALIST, ARTIST, POET
POUND RIDGE

I'm 86... really, I'm 87, but I make myself one year older. I don't want to look younger or be younger.

Recently, I ripped a bit of my earlobe. When I went to fix it, I asked, 'How much would it cost to have a face lift?' The doctor said, '$15,000 dollars.' Of course, I would never do that. I only wanted to know the price. Wouldn't it be nice if, when people die, it's just like leaves falling in the fall, but then in the spring everyone becomes beautiful and new? That would be lovely. But it doesn't happen.

We are living in this crazy period of superficiality. Old people always say, 'It was so wonderful in the 1920s, or in the 1960s.' And it was. I could approach Miles Davis, I hung out with Louis Armstrong, or I could photograph Kennedy. That's impossible today. There are a thousand photographers taking the same picture.

My style is no style.
I become more primitive
by the moment.

Right now, I have hundreds of people who would like to add me on this fucking Facebook. And I am on it because I want to see what the children of my friends are doing. I can't answer all these people who want to be my friends. What is so sad is that one doesn't keep up with old friends. I wrote a letter to the creepy owner about how he has ruined friendship.

I'm more and more in disagreement with what is happening in our culture. I have a solution for world peace. I would take the Queen Elizabeth, put every politician on it, and sink it in the Atlantic Ocean.

I was diagnosed with breast cancer (which I have a feeling never happened). They can make mistakes with diagnostics. I had a feeling it was just a benign thing. And there's all these bullshit doctors with their, 'Let's invent a drug for this and for that.' It's business. But I was radical, and I removed my breasts. I didn't want reconstruction.

The first thing I do in the morning is put my war paint on. I favor right now the look of a madame in a whore house. But who cares at this point. It's what I am, not what I look like.

I feel beautiful inside. And I'm happy to be who I am. I feel good because I do little things for people directly.

I have a gardener who's Guatemalan and he has a boy he hasn't seen in ten years. He's in touch with him every day by telephone. And in the winter he has no money, so I lend him money, which he religiously gives back to me in the spring. These are little gestures that I'm happy to be able to do. I can't do big things, but I have been nice. Each time you do something like that, you feel good about yourself. I don't have big dreams of being a super-star. I know people who had everything under the sun who committed suicide. I believe you should have only the money you need for subsistence, and that you should end your life without possessions.

Sometimes I feel good in the morning, sometimes I don't feel good. But if you take each moment and say, 'This is the end ... this is the beginning ... ' you're conflicted. You can't change destiny. We have a housekeeper who often says, 'Be careful.' Well, it's an empty word. Because things happen in spite of you being perfect.

Christina Perri

I have difficulty feeling I'm beautiful. But I love myself in all different ways. Allowing myself to have this journey that I'm on, and to keep being brave, translates to love for me.

Bailey Roberts

I'm 6'2" and a size 12. My physical stature next to somebody else is a lot. But my body is also my connection to my family. My body is my dad, it's my sister. My father always says, 'Stand up straight, be strong, remember the woman you are.' I wouldn't trade it for the world.

Petra Collins

In shaving ads, there's no hair. They're shaving nothing. Why do I buy things to get rid of something my body is trying to grow?

Not shaving was the first step toward accepting my body for what it is.

Marie Southard Ospina

I use the word 'fat' a lot in my writing. People's initial reaction is, 'You're not fat, you're beautiful,' and that in and of itself is problematic because it implies that you can't be fat and beautiful.

I am the fattest I've ever been, but I also feel like the prettiest that I've ever been. I feel like the fat is bringing something to my femininity, it's not detracting from it.

Staceyann Chin

**POET, ACTIVIST, PERFORMANCE ARTIST
BROOKLYN**

Growing up as a girl, there was such a preoccupation with whether my dress was too short. There always seemed to be multiple layers and rules between my vagina and the world.

I want to fight for a world where we have the freedom to choose to take off or put on our clothes without fearing for our safety.

I left Jamaica when I was 24 because it was too difficult to be gay there. When I came out as a lesbian, I got sexually assaulted by boys in a bathroom on my university campus. On some sick level, it was an attempt to convert me to straightness. They have a term for it—'corrective rape.' It's tied up with patriarchy, power, and your body belonging to the gaze of men.

I couldn't imagine a life without partnership with women, so I came to the U.S. to seek that. I found here the freedom to be a lesbian, particularly in New York City. But I also discovered the dissonance of being black in America. I became a poet and started to voice my dissatisfaction with the nexus that I landed in. Call me idealistic but I am gunning for utopia.

Insecurity sells. What would the fashion industry be like if every woman liked how she looked?

I'm very proud of my eczema elbows and my C-section scar and of this vagina that has survived so many difficult places but still has the inclination to pleasure.

My body allows me to continue interrupting and speaking loudly in places where motherfuckers don't want to hear it, interrupting people's ideas of beauty.

247

Tallulah
Willis

PROFESSIONAL DOODLER
LOS ANGELES

I always say, 'You know the feeling you're supposed to have on your wedding day, that you feel like a princess? Why not have that everyday?'

I struggled a lot when I was younger. I was diagnosed with body dysmorphia from reading the stupid fucking tabloids that were calling me ugly.

My biggest insecurity became my face. Because of the position I was born into, I would read these things on the internet, and think: Why would someone write that if there wasn't some truth there? I felt like I was ugly. I believed the strangers more than the people who loved me. So I thought, 'Okay, I've got a good body and that's attractive to people—I'll use that.' It made me start to dress to show off those things that weren't getting negative attention. So I would wear denim short shorts and pushup bras so that my boobs were up to my neck. I thought this will make up for what I'm lacking in my face. It was something I never wanted to say out loud because the reality was rippingly painful. It pretty much plagued me since I was thirteen years old.

I remember once during that time putting on a shirt buttoned up to the neck and having on long pants that weren't tight, and feeling so beautiful. That was a mind-fuck for me, because I never liked all the attention on my face.

It's crazy to actually like yourself, not just like the way you look, but to actually like yourself.

Eventually I was able to free myself from all that self-hate.

Sometimes I still feel vulnerable at events when there are a ton of photos being taken and I'm standing next to someone who might not have all the same insecurities I do and all I can think of is, 'What are they going to say about me?

Is it going to be this awful thing tomorrow that I have to look at and I shouldn't be looking at, but I am going to look at?'

But I believe that I have something to say and I don't need to be drunk, naked, and 'the life of the party.' It's crazy to actually like yourself, not just like the way you look, but to actually like yourself.

Domino
Kirke

Growing up in New York, I felt like I was just a body. I grew up around celebrities and people in the fashion industry. I was overly aware of people looking at me and I felt like I had to perform, or be a shell of myself, to fit in. I had a hard time getting dressed up and putting on lipstick and high heels. I'd try, but I always felt very uncomfortable.

I'm a truth seeker; I'm obsessed with being comfortable and being honest.

Vulnerability is beautiful; the older I get the more I feel comfortable with that. I feel less like I'm hiding.

Trae
Harris

Lea DeLaria

COMEDIAN, ACTOR, MUSICIAN
BROOKLYN

My entire life has been trying to put a positive spin on what it is to be butch.

The media has portrayed us as fat and stupid — we beat our wives, we cause fights, and we drive trucks.

Butches do everything. We cook, we clean, and we have to be really good at everything. And, of course, you have to take care of your lady — your femme. You have to be attentive and open doors. I've always considered myself a feminist. When I open a door for a woman, I'm not implying that she's weak in any way. To me, it's a matter of politeness and respect.

I started doing standup comedy in 1982, I've always been moderately famous. I used to say that it's been a long climb to the middle. Then, in 1993, I did the Arsenio Hall Show and became the first openly gay comic on television. In those days, standup comedy was a big activist tool.

Gay people have used a sense of humor for a very long time to survive. I'm grateful for it because I probably would have put a gun in my mouth if I didn't have that, especially after twelve years of Catholic school, where it was like everything's my fault.

When you're queer and you get home at the end of the day, and close the door, there's a part of you that goes: 'Phew... I made it. Nobody beat me up and nobody called me a dyke on the street. Today was a good day.'

My coming out experience was very very difficult. At the time, being gay was still considered a mental disease. I was cowering in the closet, terrified that someone would know my dirty little secret. It was a really difficult thing for me to accept that I was this person.

When my fiancé looks at me with this look in her eye, and I can see that she's completely and utterly in love with me, it makes me feel really handsome. Even when she's mad, I can still see it in her eyes.

So often, 'cunt' is used negatively. It's my mission to turn it into a positive word. I actually started a little hashtag — #totescunt — for when something's really good. I love a cunt! Who doesn't love a cunt?

Nathalie
Kelley

Beauty has nothing to do with the external. It's how you walk in life. How are your interactions with others? Are you quick to anger or are you quick to forgive? There are a lot of ways you can be beautiful and there are a lot of ways you can be ugly.

Georgia Pratt

It's frustrating because people are made to feel unsure about themselves because of a lack of commercial options. I was 17 and had massive boobs and I remember being very confused about how I should dress. Several years ago I couldn't find a bathing suit that fit me, so I just didn't buy one for a few years and wore underwear instead.

257

People think that beauty opens doors, but it can open doors to cliff edges

Caitlin Stasey

ACTOR, WRITER
LOS ANGELES

I was doing a film and was sharing a dressing room with my partner. Another actor saw that we were in the dressing room together and asked, 'Where do I get one of those?' I thought, 'One of what? A person? A me?' The director replied, 'Oh yeah, every dressing room comes with a pretty girl.'

As a white woman, I can turn on the television and see my physical self represented. But it's often in a form that's so contrived and sexualized. Some of the greatest female heroines have been born in the hearts and minds of men. If you're beautiful, you're objectified. If you're not beautiful, you're dismissed. The world might be more available to those who are beautiful, but it's because of criteria that weren't decided by her.

Once Jessica Biel said something like, 'I only get cast as a beautiful woman.' Everyone told her, 'Go fuck yourself, it's so hard to be a beautiful woman.' Because of moments like that, a lot of women in the same position feel like they can't ask for better roles because people are going to think they're arrogant. Maybe representation of women in film is not the most pressing issue in the world, but it's part of a wide pool of oppression. It's a trickle-down effect of a systemic and structural issue that betrays all of us.

This city is a town of women who've been told that their value is in how tight their skin is, how high their tits sit, and how their asses sit.

The people I identify with are the people who look happy and confident.

259

Mari
Malek

HUMANITARIAN, MODEL
NEW YORK

If I'm going to be a model, I have to be a model with a purpose.

I'm from South Sudan. In the village where I was born, people walked around naked, decorated in beautiful tribal jewelry and makeup. It definitely helped me be more confident with my body, at least when I was back home. But when I came to America, I didn't feel that confident.

I was born during the second civil war in Sudan. There was a lot of discrimination happening against darker-skinned people and Christian people. We, the darker skinned people, were enslaved and killed in a genocide. My whole family—I have more 20 sisters and brothers—lived together in my home. Me, my mother, and my two sisters left and ended up all alone in Egypt. We basically disappeared and left everything behind.

Create Your own Definition of Beauty

The Egyptians teased and discriminated against us because we were black, we were the darker people. Grown adult Egyptians—both men and women—made us get up from our seats so that they could sit down. Sometimes everyone would throw things at us from the windows and spit on us.

My mom found some relatives in San Diego and we moved there. But the discrimination was even worse. Now it came from people who were like us — black people.

I was in a school that was mostly black, Hispanic, and a little bit white. We were made to feel so bad about the darkness of our skin. It got to the point where some of us secretly thought about bleaching our skin to become lighter.

What helped me look at myself differently was getting into the fashion industry. My ugly dark skin that had been made fun of was suddenly so fabulous. But then I realized that there were so many superficial people. I was told, 'Hey, you're a black Sudanese girl! We're going to have you look like Alek Wek.' Basically, every Sudanese girl had to look like the supermodel Alek Wek and every black girl had to look like the supermodel Chanel Iman. I needed to stand up and be seen so I started my own agency.

We are in a world where we've been conditioned to be fearful. But maybe we should say FUCK FEAR. It's time for the world to look at one another as a human race and not as a black race or a white race. It's time for us to stop thinking that you and I are totally different people and that you are not my problem. Actually, yes, you are my problem.

We are all human, we bleed the same, we're born the same, and we die the same.

Now I use aspects of the modeling and the DJ worlds to create awareness for my country, South Sudan.

You have to be you and magic will happen. By treating my body like a temple, I met my husband. I was celibate for a year and I was mentally accepting that my soulmate or twin flame does exist.

When I started to know my own worth, I started to manifest what was worthy of me.

Clémentine Desseaux

Even though I'm a model I'm not really what you see on the campaign pictures... I'm just me everyday with pimples and cellulite

Jacky O'Shaughnessy

A few years ago, I was dyeing my hair, and I had the Dr. Kildare gloves on and the dye, and suddenly I thought, 'I am so done with this.'

Melanie Gaydos

ACTRESS, MODEL
NEW YORK

For me, beauty is more of a feeling and a state of being.

Hopefully, my style says that I'm cool, comfortable, and creative. I used to have forty different wigs — human hair, synthetic, all sorts of colors and styles. But the minute I came home and was with my close friends, I'd automatically take my wig off. So, I stopped wearing wigs about four years ago. I wore them only for societal purposes and to blend in.

I have to remember that when someone judges me in a certain way, it's a reflection of their own issues.

I was born with the genetic disorder ectodermal dysplasia. It affects the dermal layer of skin, so it affects your pores, your hair, your teeth, and your nails. It's an umbrella term for a lot of different disorders. When I was younger, I was in the hospital a lot. I had 30 to 40 surgeries.

I also didn't have a good family environment. There was a lot of alcoholism and abuse. My ectodermal dysplasia was certainly a stimulant for all the stress I was under, but I never thought it was the main cause — it was just the icing on the cake to make everything worse. Growing up, I never thought I'd be alive past the age of eighteen.

Some of my happiest moments are modeling.

I think lots of people judge me or think I'm pretty weird when they meet me for the first time. When I go on a photo shoot, the other industry models don't know what to make of me. It's difficult for me in the fashion world. People think of me as a gimmick or that I'm just being exploited for my differences. People have to talk to me to get know me in order to see where I'm coming from.

My interactions with people are stressful. We're all mirrors to each other, and I think a lot of people tend to project their bullshit on me. The things that make me different from other people are painful and scary to them. They don't understand it, so it makes them feel uncomfortable. I have to remember that when someone judges me in a certain way, it's a reflection of their own issues.

I didn't think I would kill myself, just that it would happen by accident. As I got older, though, I did think of killing myself. But I could never bring myself to do it.

Even though I didn't feel there was any point to living, I knew there was no point to killing myself. I'd rather experience life as it is right now.

Last year, I was one of the 'top 25 ugliest celebrities' in some Russian newspaper.

When I first started modeling, the word 'ugly' was always attached to me before beauty. Now (and maybe it's just what I choose to pay attention to) the word 'beauty' is often associated with my modeling. Some of my happiest moments are modeling. I love it; it's a time for me to be completely open. It's a therapeutic process for me.

I feel like I'm the only person who can deal with what I've been through and I wouldn't wish what I've experienced on anyone else.

If I'd been born without a cleft palate and with a full head of hair, I think I would be really boring. Even though I've been through a lot, they're my experiences, and I like where they've brought me today.

Acknowledgments:

To Louis, our son and brother, whose moral support and comedic relief continue to give us strength every day: The messages of this book would not have come to life without your brilliant editing skills. In addition, your choice of the cutest, tiniest rescue dogs has provided us with the maternal distraction we've needed over the years.

To Ramona, who has been our rock since 2009 when she responded to our Craigslist ad for an intern: We'll never forget when you entered our walk-up on Avenue B wearing your monster turquoise cuff from your dad. Like him, you have truly rolled up your sleeves in the name of what you believe in. There has never been a job that you wouldn't take on, and your impeccable casting skills have filled the pages of this book with the most incredible humans, whom we feel so lucky to now know.

To Tim, our husband and dad: From cooking for our team on any given night at 10 p.m. to aiding us with your lawyerly expertise and preventing us from signing our lives away to letting us tag along on your business trips so that we could afford to interview people in different states or countries, you have been the quiet, humble backbone to this organization and to our vulnerabilities. For that, we are forever indebted to you.

To everyone whom we have ever had the privilege of interviewing: Thank you for bravely opening your hearts up to us and allowing us to hold your stories. Your courage has healed both of us and millions of others, and without each of you there would be no StyleLikeU. You are rock stars.

To everyone who has ever contributed to our team: Thank you for sacrificing the security of a corporate job in order to propel this mission forward. You are true revolutionaries and we will never forget any of you.

To Ellen, our editor, whose passion for this project has fueled us every step of the way: Thank you allowing us the freedom to express our wildest visions, and for your patience with our bickering at one another during layout reviews. To Katherine and Candice, our designers: You nailed our vision visually in a way we never thought possible! For that, we cannot thank you enough.

To Olivia and Sloan: You are genius photographers to have been able to take a portrait of us that we like.

And, perhaps most of all, to our fans: StyleLikeU goes left while everyone else goes right and you noticed. Your comments, letters, and messages have been an undying light for us in our darkest and most trying times. You are the change.

First published in the United States of America in 2017 by Rizzoli International Publications, Inc. 300 Park Avenue South New York, NY 10010 www.rizzoliusa.com

Book design: Katherine Irwin and Candice Ralph

Editor: Ellen Nidy

Design Coordinators: Kayleigh Jankowski and Claudia Marina

ISBN-13: 978-0-7893-3286-8

Library of Congress Control Number: 2016961623

Printed and bound in China

Distributed to the U.S. trade by Random House